The Patent Guidebook

John T. Pienkos

The materials contained herein represent the opinions of the authors and editors and should not be construed to be the action of either the American Bar Association or the Section of Business Law unless adopted pursuant to the bylaws of the Association.

Nothing contained in this book is to be considered as the rendering of legal advice for specific cases, and readers are responsible for obtaining such advice from their own legal counsel. This book and any forms and agreements herein are intended for educational and informational purposes only.

© 2004 by the American Bar Association. All rights reserved.

No part of the publication may be reproduced, stored in a retrieval system, or transmitted in any form or by any means, electronic, mechanical, photocopying, recording, or otherwise, without the prior written permission of the publisher. Permission requests should be sent to the American Bar Association Copyrights & Contracts Department via e-mail at copyright@abanet.org or via fax at (312) 988-6030.

Printed in the United States of America.

Library of Congress Cataloging-in-Publication Data

Pienkos, John T.
The patent guidebook / by John T. Pienkos.
   p. cm.
ISBN 1-59031-444-1
  1. Patent laws and legislation—United States—Popular works. I. Title.
KF3114.6.P54 2004
346.7304'86—dc22   2004022599

Discounts are available for books ordered in bulk. Special consideration is given to state and local bars, CLE programs, and other bar-related organizations. Inquire at Book Publishing, American Bar Association, 321 North Clark Street, Chicago, IL 60610.

08   07   06   05   04   5   4   3   2   1

"To my wife Nicole"

Contents

Acknowledgments	ix
Foreword	x
Chapter 1: What Is a Patent?	1
A. Definition of a Patent	1
B. The Patent System	2
1. In the United States	2
a. The Rationale for Patents	2
b. The United States Patent and Trademark Office	3
c. Components of the Patent Law	4
d. Resolution of Patent Disputes in the Patent Office and the Courts	6
2. Outside of the United States	6
a. Patent Cooperation Treaty	7
b. Regional Patents and Patent Systems	9
C. Types of United States Patents and Patent Applications	9
D. Parts of a Utility Patent/Patent Application	11
1. Specification	11
a. Enablement	12
b. Best Mode	12
2. Drawings	12
3. Claims	13
a. Claim Limitations	13
b. Independent and Dependent Claims	14
c. Types of Claims	14

d. Special Language Including Transitional Terms and Means Clauses	15
4. Abstract and Title	16
E. Scope of a Patent	16
1. Patent Term	16
a. 20 Years from Filing	17
b. Patent Term Adjustment (PTA)	18
c. Publication and Provisional Rights	18
2. Geographic Scope	19
3. Claimed Subject Matter	19
F. Ownership of a Patent	20
1. Inventor Is Original Owner	20
2. Assignment	20
3. Joint Inventors/Joint Development	21
Chapter 2: Why Acquire a Patent?	**23**
A. Patents Provide Competitive Advantage	23
1. Assertion	24
2. Licensing	24
3. Cross-Licensing	25
4. Passive Protection, Preemptive Strikes, and Pioneering Patents	25
B. Patents as a Product	26
1. Licensing	26
a. Types of Licensing	27
2. Sale	28
3. Patent Rights in Finance and Marketing	28
C. Patent Valuation	29
1. Market Valuation	29
2. Income Valuation	30
3. Cost Valuation	32
4. What Is a Patent Really Worth?	32
D. Portfolio Strategy	33
1. Enhancement of Competitive Advantage	33
2. Enhancement of Patents As a Product	34
3. Filling in the Gaps	34
4. Dominant and Subordinate Patents	35
5. Claim Diversification	36
E. Patents in Comparison With Other Types of Intellectual Property	37
1. Patents in Comparison With Trade Secrets	37

2. Patents in Comparison With Copyrights		37
3. Patents in Comparison With Source Designation Assets		38
4. Other Forms of Intellectual Property		39

Chapter 3: What Is Patentable?   41

A. The Definition of a Patentable Invention	41
1. Patentable Subject Matter	42
2. Utility	42
3. Novelty and Prior Art	42
a. Prior Art Arising Because of Prior Invention by Another	43
b. Statutory Drop-Dead Bar Dates	43
c. Priority	45
d. Absolute Novelty Bars	45
4. Nonobviousness	46
5. Double Patenting	48
B. Computer Software, Internet-Related Innovations, and Business Methods as Patentable Subject Matter	48
1. Modern Case Law Concerning Computer-Related Inventions and Reactions by Congress and the Patent Office	49
a. State Street Bank	49
b. Reactions to State Street Bank	50
c. Response by Congress in AIPA	51
d. Response by the Patent Office	52
e. Trends in Business Method Patents	53
2. Examples of Patents Relating to Computer Software, the Internet/E-commerce, and Business Methods	54
a. Computer Software Patents	55
b. Business Method Patents	56
c. Internet/E-commerce Patents	57

Chapter 4: Obtaining and Using Your Patent   59

A. Before You Apply for a Patent	59
1. Disclosure and Confidentiality Agreements	59
2. Recording Your Work	60
3. Diligence	61
4. Prior Art Searches	62
5. Deciding Whether to Go Ahead	63
B. Applying for a Patent	64

1. Preparation of a Patent Application		64
a. Choosing What Type of Patent Application to File		65
b. Preparing the Patent Application		66
c. Time and Costs of Preparing a Patent Application		68
2. Prosecution of a Utility Patent Application		68
a. Filing a Patent Application and Related Formal Documents		68
b. Duty of Disclosure		70
c. Standard Prosecution Process		70
d. Extraordinary Measures		73
e. Prosecution History		74
f. Time and Costs of Prosecution		74
3. Important Things to Consider Before Your Patent Is Granted		75
a. Do You Still Want This Patent?		76
b. Continuing Patent Applications		76
C. Maintaining Your Patent Rights		76
1. Payment of Maintenance Fees		77
2. Fixing Problems in a Patent by Correction or Reissue		77
3. Obtaining Reaffirmation of a Patent Through Reexamination		78
4. Rebutting Challenges to a Patent		79
D. Exercising Your Patent Rights		80
1. Determining Patent Scope and Infringement		80
a. Claim Coverage and Literal Infringement		81
b. Infringement Under the Doctrine of Equivalents		81
c. Contributory Infringement, Inducement and Other Types of Infringement		82
2. Licensing, Sale, or Other Transfer of Your Patent Rights		83
3. Enforcing Your Patent Rights		84
a. Notice to Others		85
b. The Court System for Patent Matters		85
c. Laches		86
d. Risks of Patent Litigation		86

Glossary   **89**

Acknowledgements

Authors depend on a variety of sources, which serve as a foundation for what is eventually written. This publication is no exception and derives from a number of primary and secondary sources, including the patent statutes, case law, the Code of Federal Regulations, the Manual of Patent Examining Procedure, various treatises such as Patents and the Federal Circuit by Robert L. Harmon, numerous articles, other literature reviewed by the author, and lectures attended by the author during his years at Harvard Law School and in private practice. In particular, the author wishes to express his gratitude to his colleagues, and to Carl R. Schwartz in particular, with whom he has had many helpful conversations.

Foreword

The following work is intended to serve as a basic manual for executives and others who are interested in gaining a general understanding of utility patents, the patent law, and the patent system. Given the intended audience, I have attempted to balance two goals that are not always easy to reconcile: providing sufficient information to be accurate and, at the same time, not getting bogged down in so much detail as to undermine readability or bore the reader.

In attempting to achieve these two goals, I have broken up the subject matter into four chapters. Chapter 1 provides a general overview of patents and the patent system, so that the reader gets an immediate "lay of the land." After providing this general overview, I then focus in Chapter 2 upon the uses and value of patents. I chose to address this topic before delving into more of the complicated patent-related subject matter because I think it to be only natural that a person would want to have some sense of why patents are worth obtaining before investing any more time into learning about patents.

Chapter 3 discusses in greater detail the patent law concerning what is patentable. Some focus is placed in this chapter upon recent changes in the patent law concerning computer-related inventions and business method inventions, which have been the subject of significant controversy in recent times. Several examples of patents concerning inventions in these areas are also discussed. Finally, Chapter 4 addresses in greater detail the patenting process, both in terms of obtaining a patent and in terms of exercising one's patent rights.

CHAPTER **1**

What Is a Patent?

A. Definition of a Patent

A "patent" is a document that defines the scope of patent rights to exclude others from making, using, or selling an invention that is the subject of the patent. As such, a patent is like a property deed that sets forth a real property right. Just as title to a piece of land, as set forth in a deed, allows the owner to exclude others from using that land, patent rights as set forth in a patent allow its owner to exclude others from using an inventive idea.

Pursuing this analogy a little farther, two more qualities of a patent become apparent. Just as a real property right is something that is guaranteed by the government, and is only valuable to the extent that the government (or society) recognizes and enforces it, a patent right also is something that depends upon government recognition and enforcement for its value.

Also, like real property rights, patent rights have two faces. A real property right can be looked upon as both a "negative" right and a "positive" right, since it can be looked upon both as the right of the owner to be free from others' use of the property at issue, and as the right to receive positive payment from others if they do use that property (e.g., in the form of an easement). Similarly, a patent right can provide freedom from others' use of the patented invention, and also provide a right to receive compensation from anyone who does use that invention.

B. The Patent System

The U.S. patent system in many ways is the most commercially significant and well-developed national patent system in the world. Nevertheless, most of the countries around the world now have their own patent, or more generally, intellectual property or "industrial property" laws allowing for the recognition of patent rights. Certain international agreements, particularly the Patent Cooperation Treaty (PCT), which entered into force in the U.S. in 1978, and the General Agreement on Trade and Tariffs (GATT) Uruguay Round agreement of 1995, have helped harmonize to a greater extent the patent laws of many of these countries, including the United States. Yet there still does not exist any such thing as a "worldwide patent." Consequently, for U.S. businesspeople operating in a global economy, it remains important to have not only an understanding of the U.S. patent system, but also some understanding of the other, foreign and supranational patent systems that exist in the world and how those other systems interrelate with the U.S. patent system.

1. In the United States

a. The Rationale for Patents

Some foreign countries have sought to justify patents based upon the idea that ownership of one's inventions is a natural right of an inventor, in the sense that an invention is a natural extension of the inventor. Yet the justification for patents in the United States has historically been a practical one—that patents promote technological progress. This important rationale for patents is set forth in the United States Constitution, which specifies in Article I, section 8, clause 8 that Congress shall have the power to "promote the Progress of Science and useful Arts, by securing for limited Times to Authors and Inventors the exclusive Right to their respective Writings and Discoveries."

U.S. patent law thus justifies patents on the basis that patents provide a socially beneficial stimulus to develop new technologies, rather than on the basis that patents guarantee to inventors that which is naturally theirs. In order that patents provide this stimulus, the patent law accords patent rights only to those who both have invented and are willing to publicly disclose their invention. The issuing of a patent lets the whole world see what the inventor has invented, which ultimately facilitates other inventors' efforts in developing their inventions.

b. The United States Patent and Trademark Office

The U.S. patent system is a federal system that is largely managed by the U.S. Patent and Trademark Office (or simply, the "Patent Office"), particularly with respect to the issuance of patents, and largely overseen (with a few exceptions) by the U.S. federal courts. The primary roles of the Patent Office are to (1) determine whether patents should be issued based upon patent applications that are submitted to it, (2) maintain in an organized fashion records of patents that have issued and related documents, and (3) collect money for the federal government in performing these functions.

The first role of the Patent Office, determining whether patents should be issued, is its most complicated and significant role. While in some other countries patents issue simply upon the filing of patent applications by inventors, in the United States the Patent Office attempts to determine whether the inventions that are the subjects of the patent applications are actually inventive, as well as whether the patent applications meet other technical criteria. This is a key feature of the U.S. patent system, in that the Patent Office's review of patent applications prior to their issuance as patents provides the ground for a legal presumption in the U.S. that issued patents are valid.

The Patent Office performs its determination of whether patents should be issued during a process called "prosecution." For any given invention, this process generally begins upon the filing of a patent application regarding the invention in the Patent Office, and then involves a search by the Patent Office for relevant prior art (often primarily patent art), after which the Patent Office makes an initial determination of the patentability of the invention. The Patent Office often also determines whether the patent application meets other technical criteria. Although in some cases the Patent Office will already at this point find that the patent application should be issued as a patent, typically discussion and argumentation back and forth between the Patent Office and the patent applicant occur before a patent is allowed to issue.

Not uncommonly, the entire prosecution process exceeds two years. Sometimes, the prosecution process becomes extended simply due to the fact that the issue of how much patent protection should be afforded to the invention at hand is extremely complicated, or because extraordinary measures must be taken by the patent applicant before the Patent Office recognizes that a patent should be allowed to issue. Of course, the prosecution process does not always end in the issuance of a patent for some patent applications concerning inventions that the Patent Office rightly considers to be unpatentable. Nevertheless, a majority of all patent applications that are filed in the Patent Office eventually issue as patents, albeit many have lesser scope than what was originally applied for.

The Patent Office's role in determining whether a patent should be issued does not always end upon the issuance of the patent. In particular, in a few circumstances the Patent Office can reconsider its earlier decisions concerning the issuance of patents, for example, because the validity of a patent has come into question, to correct a patent, or to resolve a conflict of priority between an issued patent and a pending patent application.

The other roles of the Patent Office in maintaining patent records and collecting money are perhaps not as interesting to patent applicants, but nevertheless are critical to the operation of the patent system. Maintaining records and enabling easy access of those records by the public not only allows the public to become aware of patents that have issued, so that the public can avoid infringing those patents, but also allows other prospective inventors to ultimately capitalize off of the patented inventions in developing still new inventions (once the patents on the inventions have expired). Collecting monetary payments is critical to the patent system in that it allows the Patent Office to be a self-funding organization. Unfortunately, even this does not guarantee the financial independence and integrity of the patent system insofar as some of the money collected by the Patent Office has from time to time been taken by the federal government from the Patent Office and used instead to fund other unrelated programs!

c. Components of the Patent Law

The patent law has a federal statutory aspect, an administrative aspect and a case law aspect. That is, the patent law is first defined by the laws passed by Congress, additionally refined by administrative regulations promulgated by the Patent Office, and further interpreted by the courts in their decisions. Unlike many other types of law, the patent law is entirely federal in nature and there is no state patent law in the United States. That is, patent law statutes are only passed by the U.S. federal government, patent law regulations are only promulgated by a federal Patent Office, and the patent law is only interpreted by the federal courts and federal agencies.

The patent law statutes can be found at Title 35 of the United States Code. Title 35 has four parts. Part I of the Code concerns the establishment and operation of the Patent Office. Part II defines what is a patentable invention, and also sets forth the general features of the patent prosecution process. It is in Part II that the requirements for a patent application, including the enablement and best mode requirements, are set forth. Part III primarily concerns issued patents, and sets forth how existing patents can be corrected, reissued and reexamined by the Patent Office. Additionally, Part III sets forth the ways in which patent rights can be enforced. Part IV of Title 35 concerns the Patent Cooperation Treaty (PCT).

Title 35 gives the Director of the United States Patent and Trademark Office (generally, in consultation with a Patent Public Advisory Committee and upon providing notice and opportunity for public comment) the power to create regulations governing the operation of the Patent Office. In accordance with this statutory provision, Title 37 of the Code of Federal Regulations has been established. These regulations set forth, in greater detail than the patent law statutes, many of the exact procedures by which the Patent Office operates, and the requirements that must be met by patent applicants, patent-holders and other parties in dealing with the Patent Office. The level of detail provided by these regulations is quite specific—for example, the regulations specify the mailing addresses of the Patent Office for specific functions.

Although Title 37 sets forth the rules governing the Patent Office and interactions with the Patent Office, an additional resource called the Manual of Patent Examining Procedure (the "MPEP") has been developed by the Patent Office to further clarify for patent examiners (and others such as patent attorneys and patent applicants) the procedures of the Patent Office. Although it does not have the force of law, the MPEP nevertheless is often regarded as authoritative by Patent Office employees in performing their work and consequently has a significant impact upon the manner in which the Patent Office operates.

As in other areas of the law, many legal issues that are only ambiguously addressed, or not addressed at all, by the patent law statutes have been considered and resolved by the courts. Because the patent laws are federal laws, almost all patent cases are heard by the federal courts, in particular, the federal district courts, usually the Federal Circuit Court of Appeals for patent appeals and, if necessary, the United States Supreme Court. Many of the most significant concepts in patent law discussed elsewhere in this book, including the doctrine of equivalents and the requirement that all limitations of a claim be performed in order for there to be infringement, have been or are in the process of being clarified by such decisions.

d. Resolution of Patent Disputes in the Patent Office and the Courts

Patent disputes are resolved exclusively by way of federal entities, e.g., federal courts for most cases, the International Trade Commission (for certain import disputes), the Court of Claims (for claims against the government), and the Patent Office, rather than by local or state governmental entities. If you would like the courts to enforce your patent against an infringer, you would typically start by bringing a suit against the infringer in a federal district court. That court's decision could in turn almost always be appealed to the Federal Circuit Court of Appeals in Washington D.C. (or simply the "Federal Circuit"), which is a special appellate court that has been granted authority to decide patent appeals from federal courts, the Patent Office, the International Trade Commission, and the Court of Claims. The Federal Circuit was created as a proxy for the other federal circuit courts, so that complicated patent issues are decided in a relatively uniform manner by judges who regularly deal with and thoroughly understand the patent law. Although parties can appeal decisions by the Federal Circuit to the U.S. Supreme Court, the Supreme Court on average decides only about one significant patent case per year.

2. Outside of the United States

Most of the other nations of the world also provide patent protection in some manner. Many of these foreign patent systems differ from that of the United States in significant ways. For example, many foreign countries examine patent applications in a less rigorous manner than patent applications are examined in the United States, particularly in terms of whether the inventions described and claimed in those applications are patentable. While it may be easier for patent applicants to obtain patents in these foreign countries than it is in the United States, the patents that are issued do not carry a strong presumption that the patents are actually valid.

In the past, a party that wanted to obtain patents in multiple countries had to independently file separate patent applications in each of those countries (except in special cases), and all of the patent applications had to be filed within 12 months of the earliest filing date. This was particularly complicated not only in terms of the logistics of translating and sending documents to many different patent offices, but also because the requirements for patent applications and filing those applications varied from country to country. Relatively recently, certain multinational patent systems have been developed that facilitate the process of applying for patents in multiple countries, both by extending the time period during which a patent applicant must decide whether to pursue patent applications in the various individual countries, and by combining portions of the patent prosecution processes of certain countries into a single process that is applicable to each of those particular countries.

a. Patent Cooperation Treaty

The Patent Cooperation Treaty (PCT), which entered into force in the U.S. in 1978, allows patent applicants from PCT member nations to preserve the option to apply for patent applications in almost 110 nations all at once through the filing of a single PCT patent application. A PCT patent application can be filed by submitting it to the corresponding patent office of the patent applicant's home country (among other places). In a request form attached to the PCT patent application, the patent applicant indicates those of the member nations in which the patent applicant intends to (or possibly intends to) eventually pursue patents. Once the PCT patent application is filed, it enters "Chapter I" of an "international stage" of prosecution in which an International Searching Authority conducts a search for prior art relating to the patent application. The information that is found is explained in a search report prepared by the International Searching Authority, which is then sent to the patent applicant. After the search report has been provided, an International Bureau publishes the PCT patent application. Publication normally occurs shortly after 18 months have passed since the filing date of the PCT patent application.

At month 19 after the filing date of the PCT patent application, the patent applicant has an option whether to enter "Chapter II" of the international stage. By choosing to enter Chapter II, the patent applicant causes an International Preliminary Examining Authority to prepare an International Preliminary Examination Report that is a nonbinding statement of whether the patent application should be allowed to issue as a patent in view of the prior art. Then, at about month 30 (a few countries permit more delays) after the filing date of the PCT patent application, the patent applicant must determine whether to enter the "national stage" of prosecution, that is, determine whether it is still desired to pursue patent applications in any of the individual nations that were originally selected when the PCT patent application was filed. Sometimes, based upon the search report provided by the International Searching Authority and/or any International Preliminary Examination Report, the patent applicant will decide that it is not worthwhile to continue to pursue patent applications in one or more of the countries that were originally selected. Under a recent change to the PCT rules, the patent applicant alternatively can wait up to 30 months after the filing date of the PCT patent application to decide whether to enter the national stage even when the patent applicant decides not to enter Chapter II.

Assuming that the patent applicant does wish to go forward with patent applications in at least some of the countries that were originally selected, the patent applicant by the 30-month date must provide additional filing fees and translations of the patent application to the patent offices of the countries in which patent applications are to be pursued (albeit, as discussed below, for a European patent application, a patent application in English will suffice until allowance). Once the national stage is begun in one or more countries, the prosecution process proceeds with respect to those individual countries as if the patent applicant had initially filed separate patent applications in those countries. However, to the extent that an International Preliminary Examination Report was obtained, the national patent offices of some countries may largely base their initial decisions on whether to allow their respective patent applications to issue as patents upon that report. Thus, in addition to providing a simplified route by which patent applicants can begin to pursue patent applications in multiple countries and delaying the time at which the patent applicants must decide whether to pursue patents in those different countries, the PCT patent system also can provide meaningful information to patent applicants that can help the patent applicants decide whether and where to pursue patents.

b. Regional Patents and Patent Systems

Aside from the PCT patent system, certain regional patent systems have also emerged, including the European patent system covering many of the nations of Europe (including the United Kingdom, France and Germany), a patent system for nations that formerly made up the Soviet Union, particularly Russia, and a patent system for some of the states within Africa. The foremost of these regional patent systems is the European patent system, because of the degree to which this patent system integrates the patent systems of many of the European countries, the economic significance of Europe in the world economy, and the relative enforceability and strength of the patents that this system produces.

By filing a single patent application in the European Patent Office, a patent applicant starts a prosecution process that can be applicable toward the obtaining of a patent in each of the European states covered by the European patent system. That is, the prosecution process does not have to be repeated with respect to each individual nation. For this reason, the European patent system more fully integrates the patenting process of its member states than does the PCT patent system, which only provides a preliminary search (and sometimes a preliminary examination) before turning over the prosecution process to its individual member states (or corresponding regional patent systems). Of further benefit to U.S. patent applicants is that the patent prosecution process in the European patent system can take place in English up until allowance of the patent application, thereby minimizing the costs and difficulty of the prosecution process.

C. Types of United States Patents and Patent Applications

While the above discussion may suggest that the U.S. patent system only involves a single type of patent application and a single type of patent, that is not true. The Patent Office actually is able to issue three types of patents, namely "utility patents," "design patents" and "plant patents." Utility patents are what many commonly think of as patents, and relate to inventions having a new utilitarian aspect. Inventions protected by utility patents may concern any new and useful process, machine, manufacture, or composition of matter, or any new and useful improvement thereof. In contrast, design patents concern new external ornamental designs. As for plant patents, these patents are limited to inventions of new species of asexually reproduced plants. Because utility patents are the patents that are obtained for new technological innovations including innovations involving business methods, our discussion of patents throughout the remainder of this book will be limited to only this type of patent.

Even though we will narrow our focus to one type of patent, namely utility patents, we cannot so easily narrow our focus to one type of utility patent application. Most commonly, inventors wishing to obtain utility patents on their inventions begin the prosecution process by filing utility (or "regular") patent applications on their inventions. However, the patent laws were modified in 1995 to allow also for the filing of a simplified patent application, the "provisional" patent application. Such an application, once filed, merely places an invention on record in the Patent Office and becomes abandoned if nothing more is done by the patent applicant within one year of the filing of the patent application. Although provisional patent applications lack viability in comparison with utility patent applications in that provisional patent applications cannot by themselves issue as patents, there nevertheless are certain circumstances in which it makes sense for a patent applicant to file a provisional patent application rather than a utility patent application (as discussed further in Chapter 4).

Additionally, the U.S. patent system also recognizes continuing patent applications. These patent applications can arise regarding a particular invention only after another utility patent application has already been filed. That is, each of these patent applications is based upon one or more earlier, parent patent applications.

Continuing patent applications in particular include three types of patent applications, simple continuation applications, continuation-in-part applications, and divisional applications. A continuation application is simply a new patent application that adds no new information relative to its parent application and generally claims the same invention. A continuation-in-part application is a new patent application that, in addition to retaining information from its parent application, also adds new information. A divisional application is a new patent application that includes the same information as its parent, but claims only a portion of the subject matter of the parent. Often, but not necessarily, a divisional application comes into existence because the Patent

Office decides that the parent application concerns more than one invention and consequently requires a "dividing off" of one invention from the other.

D. Parts of a Utility Patent/Patent Application

Although U.S. utility patents (and patent applications) can vary to some extent in their form and length, many utility patents have the following parts.

1. Specification

The specification in a utility patent is the written portion of the patent. It includes a written description, one or more claims, an abstract and a title. Although technically forming part of the specification, the claims, abstract and title of a patent serve specialized purposes within the patent, and consequently are discussed separately in more detail below.

The specification typically includes several sections that form the written description of the invention. First among these is a background section, in which the general state of the art, and the rationale or need for the invention, are described. To the extent that the background section sets forth the rationale for the invention, this section can be important during the prosecution process and afterward as a justification for the patentability of the invention. The background section will sometimes also include a statement of the general field of the invention.

The specification also includes a summary of the invention. The summary of the invention is a brief statement of key features and/or advantages of the invention. Often, the summary of the invention will closely parallel the broadest claims of the patent. Further, when drawings are present in a patent, the specification includes a brief description of the drawings.

The main body of the written description is the detailed description section, in which one or more embodiments of the invention are methodically set forth with great detail. Often, the detailed description section discusses, one by one, the different drawings in the patent application, although patents can vary considerably from this format.

a. Enablement

For a patent to be valid under the patent laws, the patent must set forth the invention in sufficient detail that someone of "ordinary skill in the art" of the invention would be able to make and use the invention. The bare minimum required for a patent description to be enabling for one of ordinary skill in the art is often a difficult question to answer, and consequently inventions are sometimes disclosed in far greater detail than is necessary to be enabling.

b. Best Mode

Additionally for a patent to be valid under the patent laws, the patent must at least disclose the preferred attributes and operation of the invention, or the invention's "best mode." This requirement exists to prevent inventors from hiding their most preferred techniques. Such behavior on the part of inventors would undermine the social-benefit rationale for the patent laws, since such behavior could result in the granting of patent rights to inventors even though those inventors had not revealed their full invention to the public.

2. Drawings

Although drawings are often absent from patent applications concerning chemical compounds or biotechnology-related inventions (which may use sequence listings or deposits of biological material to describe the inventions), drawings are nevertheless needed in many patent applications to explain the inventions. Depending upon the invention, the drawings in a patent application can take a variety of forms, ranging from physical pictures or schematics, to graphs and flow charts. Business method patents in particular often employ flow charts to show steps of the invented method or process. The drawings in a patent commonly provide the framework for the detailed description section of the specification, and different components shown in the drawings are typically labeled by numbers or other identifying marks.

3. Claims

The claims are the core of a patent in that they define in precise, legalistic language the invention to which patent rights have been accorded to the inventor or owner of the patent. The claims of a patent are often compared to the language of a property deed in that they set forth the "metes and bounds" of an invention much like the property deed sets forth the metes and bounds of real property. Nevertheless, because claim language is legalistic, terse and complicated, and because of the complexity of most inventions, the specification and drawings of a patent usually are necessary for understanding the invention encompassed by the patent. Indeed, claims are often interpreted based upon the specification and drawings where ambiguities exist.

a. Claim Limitations

Each claim of a patent recites a number of distinct (or relatively distinct) aspects or characteristics of the invention. The type of aspects of the invention that are the focus of the claims can vary depending upon the nature of the invention and the way in which the invention is described. For example, in patents having to do with inventions in the mechanical arts, claims often tend to recite specific component parts or "elements" of the invention (e.g., an automobile is made up of an engine, a chassis, a passenger compartment, a drive train, wheels, etc.). Other claims focus on steps that are performed according to the invention, signals that are processed by the invention and a variety of other characteristics.

Regardless of their type, the different aspects and characteristics of an invention that are recited in a claim can respectively be understood as the "limitations" of the claim. In order for someone to "literally" infringe the claim, the purported infringer must make, use or sell (or import) something that has or does every limitation in that claim. As discussed further below, it is also possible for someone to infringe the claim under the "doctrine of equivalents" if there are only insubstantial differences between the limitations of the claim and that which supposedly infringes the claim. Generally speaking, a claim can only be infringed if the alleged infringer is doing everything the claim says, or at least is doing an "equivalent" of everything the claim says.

b. Independent and Dependent Claims

Each claim of a patent is written as if it was a separate sentence describing a particular version or embodiment of the invention. The claims of a patent come in two forms—independent claims and dependent claims. Each independent claim is a sentence that stands alone. That is, each independent claim recites a number of limitations that adequately describe a particular version of the invention, without referring to any other claims.

In contrast, each dependent claim is a sentence that refers back to one or more of the other claims. All of the limitations of the claim(s) to which a dependent claim refers are considered to be included within that dependent claim. Consequently, a dependent claim always has more limitations than just those that are expressly recited in the dependent claim. The first claim of a patent should always be an independent claim, since there are no other claims preceding that first claim from which it could depend.

Most patents tend to have not many more than three independent claims, and not many more than 20 claims overall, since the Patent Office charges additional fees when the number of independent claims exceeds three or the total number of claims exceeds 20.

c. Types of Claims

Although claim language can vary widely from patent to patent, certain types of claims recur often enough to warrant special mention. When an invention is described in a claim in terms of its structural components or elements, the claim often takes the form of an "apparatus" claim or a "system" claim. That is, the claim states that what is claimed is an apparatus or a system, and then proceeds to list the various parts of the apparatus or system. When an invention is described in a claim as a process, the claim often takes the form of a "method" claim. That is, the claim states that what is claimed is a method, and then proceeds to list the various steps of operation of the invention.

d. Special Language Including Transitional Terms and Means Clauses

As mentioned, claim language is highly legalistic and uses many specialized terms. For this reason, it is almost always a good idea to have a skilled patent practitioner prepare the claims of a patent. The following are some examples of commonly used, specialized claim language.

First, a claim always begins with an introductory phrase or clause termed the "preamble." The preamble states the general subject matter of the claim, and limitations within the preamble may or may not be considered to be true limitations of the claim. The preamble is separated from the remainder of the claim by a transitional word or phrase, which typically is one of the following: "comprising," "including," "having," and "consisting of."

The first three of these transitional terms, comprising, including, and having, have a specific legal meaning—namely, that all of the limitations following the transitional word are necessarily included within the invention, but that the invention is not restricted to having those limitations alone. That is, these terms signify that the claim is open-ended in the sense that it can encompass any other limitations in addition to those that are expressly recited. In contrast, the last term, consisting of, has a specific legal meaning that the limitations following the term are the *only* limitations. That is, the term consisting of signifies that the claim is closed-ended and can only include the limitations that are expressly recited in the claim.

Although these terms—comprising, including, having and consisting of—are typically employed as the transitional word or phrase between the preamble of a claim and the rest of the claim, these terms can also be used in other locations throughout a claim. If used in such other locations, the terms retain their specialized meanings. However, while these transitional phrase rules apply within the United States, they do not necessarily apply in foreign countries (e.g., in Australia, the term "comprising" signifies that the claim is closed-ended rather than open-ended).

A further expression that is commonly used in claims and has a specialized meaning is the term "means for." When used in combination with a function (e.g., "means for communicating") the term generally denotes any structure that is described in the specification of the patent that performs the particular function and equivalents thereof. For example, a "means for communicating" might be any of a telephone, a radio, a walkie-talkie and fire for creating a smoke signal, if all of these things were disclosed in the specification of the patent. This specialized meaning of "means for" is explicitly set forth in the patent laws, and is intended to provide a linguistic mechanism by which patent applicants can have claims that more generally encompass multiple devices that perform a given function. This language can be particularly useful when an invention is made up of new parts that do not yet have commonly accepted names, or when a number of different mechanisms could perform the same function.

4. Abstract and Title

The abstract of a patent is a short section of 150 words or less that basically summarizes key inventive aspects of the patent. The abstract has no legal significance in terms of defining or restricting the patented invention. However, the abstract has practical significance insofar as it is the abstract that appears on the face of a patent, and which is often used by others to get a quick idea of what the patent is about. The abstract often plays an "Executive Summary" role, that is, provides a quick synopsis of the invention for non-patent-experts.

The title of a patent is simply that—the title on the front of the patent. Again, the title is only important insofar as it conveys a preliminary idea of what the patent is about.

E. Scope of a Patent

The scope of any given patent, though possibly quite expansive, is nevertheless restricted in several ways. In particular, a patent is limited temporally, geographically, and with respect to its subject matter.

1. Patent Term

For many years, the patent laws of the United States were very different from the patent laws of most other countries in that the U.S. patent laws provided that a patent's term lasted 17 years from the date of issuance of the patent. However, with the ratification of GATT in 1995, U.S. patent laws concerning patent term were adjusted (with a transition rule for existing patents) to conform more closely to the term applicable in most other nations.

a. 20 Years from Filing

Since June 8, 1995, the term of any United States utility patent generally lasts from the date on which the patent issued until 20 years from the filing date of the earliest utility (non-provisional) patent application that was filed in the United States to which the patent claims priority. Under normal circumstances, therefore, if you file a utility patent application concerning your invention in the United States and eventually are granted a patent based upon that patent application, your patent will expire 20 years from the day on which the patent application was filed in the Patent Office. Additionally, if you originally file a utility patent application but then file a continuing patent application based upon that first patent application, your 20-year patent term for a patent issuing from that continuing patent application is calculated based upon the filing date of the first patent application rather than the later filing date of the continuing patent application.

Provisional patent applications do not impact patent term. That is, if you originally file a provisional patent application in the United States, and then file a utility patent application based upon that provisional patent application (within one year subsequent to filing the provisional patent application), your 20-year patent term will be measured from the filing date of the utility patent application, and not be shortened by the time period in between the filing of the provisional patent application and the filing of the utility patent application.

Just because a patent's term is measured from the filing date of a corresponding patent application does not mean that patent rights exist during the entire 20-year time period following the filing date. Rather, full patent rights (not counting provisional patent rights, which are discussed below) under your patent only exist during the time between the date your patent issued as a patent and the date your patent expires. That is, the actual amount of time during which you have full patent rights depends to a great extent upon how much of your 20-year patent term was "eaten up" by the patent prosecution process in between the filing of your patent application and the issuance of your patent. Consequently, delays in the prosecution process on the part of the Patent Office (as well as on the part of you and your attorney) can shorten your eventual patent term.

b. Patent Term Adjustment (PTA)

Largely to address the aforementioned concern regarding the effect of Patent Office delays on patent term, the U.S. patent laws were recently changed under the American Inventors Protection Act (AIPA) of 1999 to provide that a patent's term can be slightly lengthened beyond the standard 20-year term under several circumstances where the patent prosecution process has become overly long due to slowness on the part of the Patent Office. For example, under the new law, a patent's term now will be lengthened (positive Patent Term Adjustment or "PTA") to account for a failure on the part of the Patent Office to take action with respect to a newly filed patent application within 14 months of the filing date. These changes to the patent laws make it more complicated to calculate the length of the term of your U.S. patent. Additionally, while the new law provides that excessive slowness on the part of the Patent Office during prosecution can add positive PTA to your patent term, excessive slowness by you (or your attorney) during the prosecution process can be doubly harmful in that such delays not only delay issuance of the patent, but also can offset any positive PTA in whole or in part.

c. Publication and Provisional Rights

AIPA also added a wrinkle to the prior rule that you had no patent rights until your U.S. patent issued. Under AIPA, patent applications filed in the United States may be published 18 months after being filed. This rule is similar to that of most foreign countries, which publish their patent applications 18 months after the first filing, and constituted a change from the previous U.S. rule that patent applications would normally remain confidential until issuing as patents. In order to provide some compensation to U.S. inventors for the loss of confidentiality, AIPA further provided that "provisional rights" exist during the intermediate period between the time your patent application is published and the later date on which it issues as a patent. That is, if certain requirements are met, and your patent application does in fact issue as a patent in substantially the form published, you can potentially collect some payment from parties who "infringed" during the intermediate period between publication of your patent application and issuance of your patent.

2. Geographic Scope

The patent rights set forth in a patent only exist within, and only can be enforced within, a particular nation-state or at most a particular region (i.e., group of nation-states) to which the patent pertains. That is, there is no such thing as a "world patent." Further, to obtain a patent for a particular country or at most a particular region, it is almost always necessary that, at some point, you file a specific patent application in that particular country or region. Although the Patent Cooperation Treaty provides a mechanism by which the right to file a patent application can be reserved in about 110 nations simultaneously by filing only a single PCT patent application, the PCT patent application eventually must be followed by filings in the patent offices of individual nations or regions (e.g., the European Patent Office) if protection in those nations or regions is desired.

3. Claimed Subject Matter

A fundamental consideration when evaluating a claim is the claim's scope or breadth. A broader claim encompasses (i.e., can be infringed by) more subject matter than a narrower claim and, for that reason, a broader claim regarding an invention is typically more valuable than a narrower claim regarding that invention.

As a general rule, a claim is broader if it uses open-ended transitional terms, rather than closed-ended transitional terms as discussed above. Further, assuming that open-ended language is used, a claim with fewer limitations is generally a broader claim than a claim with more limitations. This is because, while a claim with a first set of limitations can be infringed by anything that satisfies those limitations (or equivalents of those limitations), a claim that recites a second set of limitations in addition to the first set only can be infringed by things that satisfy all of the limitations of both sets (or equivalents of those limitations).

For example, a first claim might recite a vehicle with a headlight, while a second claim might recite a vehicle with a headlight and four wheels. In this case (assuming that the claims did not have any other limitations), the first claim reciting the single headlight would be broader than the second claim, since motorcycles with only a single headlight would be encompassed by the first claim but not the second.

F. Ownership of a Patent

1. Inventor Is Original Owner

It is generally the inventor(s) of an invention claimed in a patent (and not their employer) who own the patent unless an agreement establishing another's ownership of the patent has been executed, or unless the invention was made by the inventor(s) while employed for the specific purpose of inventing (in this situation, which is very rare, the patent is owned by the employer).

But who counts as an inventor? According to the patent laws, an inventor is a person who has conceived the invention or who has contributed to the conception of the invention. Consequently, the inventor probably will not be a person who just builds a working prototype of an invention following someone else's blueprint. Rather, the inventor need only be the person (or persons) who thought of the invention.

2. Assignment

Of course, most patent applications in the United States are pursued by companies and not independent inventors, and most patents ultimately end up belonging to companies. The usual mechanism by which the ownership of most inventions, patent applications, and patents is transferred from employee-inventors to their corporate employers is the "assignment agreement."

It is usually the case that the employment agreements between employers and employees provide that all inventions (and resulting patent applications and patents) made by the employees within the scope of their employment belong to the employer. Thus, the employment agreements serve as generalized assignment agreements by which employees essentially assign all patent rights relating to their work to their employers.

Additionally, it is also usually the case that employee-inventors execute individual confirmation assignment agreements when patent applications are filed on their respective inventions during their employment. Such an agreement, which provides a short recitation of the various patent rights that are being transferred from an employee-inventor to his or her employer, usually serves merely as a formal confirmation of the assignment of rights that occurred under the employee's employment agreement. Of course, where no employment agreement exists, or no ownership provision is made in an employment agreement, such an individual assignment agreement can be critical for establishing the employer's ownership of the patent rights in question.

An assignment agreement must be in writing and signed at least by the employee. Often, the assignment agreement is also notarized or other formal efforts are taken to authenticate and witness the document. Although a variety of agreements including employment agreements can be recorded in the Patent Office as evidence of ownership, it is usually these formal assignment agreements that are recorded in the Patent Office. By recording such an assignment (or other) agreement in the Patent Office during prosecution of a patent application to which the agreement pertains, it becomes possible for the Patent Office to list the name of the company owning the patent on the front page of the issued patent.

Another way in which patent rights can be transferred from an employee to an employer is in the form of "shop rights," which are typically created under individual states' laws. In accordance with shop rights, an employer may have limited, nonexclusive rights to make and use an invention of an employee when the employee has used in any way the resources of the company to invent the invention, even where the employer is not entitled to gain full ownership of the patent concerning the invention.

3. Joint Inventors/Joint Development

Increasingly common today are situations in which multiple inventors have collaborated on (and helped to conceive) an invention. The multiple inventors may all be employees of the same employer, or may be employed by multiple companies that have a joint development agreement. Also, one or more of the inventors may be independent contractors. Where the joint inventors are not all employed by the same company or otherwise are not part of a single umbrella organization, determining ownership can become complicated. As a general rule, each and every inventor corresponding to a patent has equal ownership of that patent absent an agreement to the contrary. Consequently, if all but one of the inventors corresponding to a given patent assign their rights to a company (e.g., their employer), but the remaining inventor does not (e.g., because that inventor is an independent consultant of the company without any duty to assign rights to that company), the company may not be able to preclude the remaining inventor from licensing the patent to others, even the company's competitors. For this reason, it is important that companies that are jointly developing new technologies with other parties clearly resolve ownership issues in their joint development agreements with those other parties in a proactive manner.

CHAPTER **2**

Why Acquire a Patent?

In the past decade, companies have become increasingly interested in patents. In particular, the number of applications for utility patents to the U.S. Patent Office rose about 80% between 1994 and 2003, and the number of utility patents issued by the U.S. Patent Office increased by about 70% over that same period. Why are companies applying and paying for all of these patents?

A. Patents Provide Competitive Advantage

From a general business perspective, companies have become increasingly interested in patents and other forms of intellectual property because patents and other intellectual property assets are sources of competitive advantage. While other, more traditional sources of competitive advantage—for example, better access to capital, labor or natural resources—have been weakened by globalization, improved financial markets and improved communication and transportation technologies, patents and other intellectual property assets have only become stronger and more defensible as a result of a variety of favorable legal changes.

While patents do not positively authorize patent-holders to use their patented inventions, patents do allow the patent-holders to prevent others from making, using or selling the patented inventions. Consequently, patents provide a way of throwing roadblocks in front of one's competitors that can prevent those competitors from taking advantage of the technologies that one is developing, or at least can provide some leverage vis-à-vis those competitors. There are several ways in which patents can be employed for this purpose.

1. Assertion

If you believe one of your competitors is making, using or selling a product or process that infringes your patent's claims, after consultation with counsel, you may decide to notify your competitor about your patent. In some circumstances, your competitor may stop its infringing behavior once it learns of the existence of your patent (and realizes that your patent's claims do actually encompass its behavior).

Of course, not all companies will stop infringing your patent just because you have informed them of its existence. On the one hand, a competitor may have legitimate reasons to believe that it is not infringing your patent even though the competitor's infringement seems clear enough to you. On the other hand, some competitors will refuse to stop infringing your patent even though they know that they should. With respect to these competitors, it may be necessary to sue them before the competitors will stop their infringing activity.

2. Licensing

Given the risks of patent litigation, it is common for parties having a patent infringement dispute to settle their dispute in the form of a license agreement in which the accused infringer agrees to pay the patent-holder royalties in exchange for being able to continue its infringing activities. The amount of royalties can vary significantly based upon a variety of considerations including the strength of the patent, the type of technology, and the relative strengths of the opposing parties. Royalty rates in the range of 3%–10% of total product sales by the licensee are common in a wide variety of circumstances, albeit in cutting-edge technologies the royalty rates may be higher.

By agreeing to a license in this type of situation, a patent-holder is only imperfectly exercising the patent-holder's patent rights, since the patent-holder is not exercising the patent rights so as to be entirely free from infringement. However, at least the patent-holder is exercising the patent rights so as to be free from infringement without compensation, and the royalties paid by the competitor are a drag on the competitor's business. This situation is somewhat analogous to a situation in which a real property owner is forced to sell his or her property to the government under eminent domain, since similarly in that situation the property owner does receive some reasonable compensation for the loss of his or her property rights (albeit, in the case of patent rights, the invader is not the government).

3. Cross-Licensing

In a few circumstances, two or more patent-holders have patents on technologies that are made, used or sold by one another. In such circumstances, the patent rights of a first patent-holder may be asserted against another patent-holder, and vice-versa, as a tit-for-tat strategy. To the extent that the first patent-holder's patent rights and those of its competitor are of roughly the same strength, the patent-holder and the competitor may grant one another the same license to their respective patent(s).

4. Passive Protection, Preemptive Strikes, and Pioneering Patents

Patents provide some protection to the patent-holder simply by being in existence. Many companies, before developing a new product or pursuing a new business, attempt to identify patents that may pose a problem for their future product/activity. Typically, upon identifying such patents, the companies take steps to avoid the patents, ranging from designing around the patents to complete abandonment of the new product/business. Thus, once a patent is obtained, it provides its patent-holder with some protective value even if the patent-holder is entirely passive (aside from doing what is necessary to keep the patent in force, e.g., paying maintenance fees).

While generally providing this protective value, patents may be particularly effective in this regard with respect to potential new entrants to a market. In contrast to existing competitors, which often have sufficient technical personnel and other resources to develop their own new technologies that are not protected by an existing patent, potential new competitors may not have (or may be more reluctant to expend) such resources. Thus, patents can act as a form of "preemptive strike" at potential new competitors.

This is even truer at times when technologies are experiencing rapid growth or entirely new technologies are emerging. At these times, inventors' innovations may be sufficiently groundbreaking that all competitors will have to use these innovations to be in the desired market. In such cases, "pioneering" patents protecting these technological breakthroughs can preclude most competition for a significant period of time, or at least guarantee the patent-holder significant royalties. Similarly, patent rights concerning innovations that are in conformance with new standards for a technology area can also be particularly valuable.

B. Patents as a Product

In addition to being viewed as a mechanism for inhibiting the competition, the patent rights provided by patents are also increasingly being viewed as assets that can be actively exercised as a revenue source for, or even constitute the primary product of, the patent-holder.

1. Licensing

Although the payment of royalties under a patent license can be viewed as the imperfect exercising of a patent-holder's right to prevent infringement of the patent-holder's patent, royalty payments can also be viewed as a positive benefit that naturally comes to a patent-holder by virtue of owning the patent. Like rent received by a property owner from a tenant, royalty payments can be looked upon as a revenue stream generated by a patent rather than simply payment that is grudgingly accepted by the patent-holder as compensation for an infringement.

Indeed, more than a few companies today have come to view technology development, combined with the obtaining and licensing of patent rights concerning their technological innovations, as their primary business purpose. Instead of manufacturing, distributing and/or retailing tangible products as their primary source of revenue, these companies originate innovations that are in turn licensed to other companies that make tangible use of those innovations. Many of these "innovation companies" are on the cutting edge of the development of new technologies for emerging industries. By obtaining patent rights with respect to these new technologies, the companies are able to set the standard for, and receive highly profitable licensing royalties from, all or virtually all other companies that make or sell products related to these emerging industries.

While some companies choose to pursue a strategy of technology development and licensing as their business focus, others are forced to pursue this strategy out of necessity. Indeed, some companies as well as other institutions do not have sufficient resources themselves to produce and market products related to their innovations, or consider such functions to be inconsistent with their organizational purpose. In this category are the many universities across the United States that have become quite successful in attempting to out-license their many patent rights concerning inventions developed by their faculty and other researchers.

Still other companies actively pursue the licensing of their patent rights not as their primary business purpose but rather because the companies have large numbers of patents that have become irrelevant to those companies from the perspective of their present business strategies. For example, IBM is now offering many of its thousands of patents for license, largely because these patents concern technologies that are no longer being utilized by IBM's products but nevertheless may be of use to other companies.

a. Types of Licensing

The type of license that a patent-holder may grant to others can depend upon a variety of factors, including the strength of the patents, the nature of and market for the patented technology, and the patent-holder's competitors in the marketplace. A variety of different licensing options are available. One type of license is the exclusive license, in which the patent-holder licenses patent rights to only one other party, the exclusive licensee, and agrees not to license patent rights to any third party. Because in this case the patent-holder is licensing patent rights only to the exclusive licensee, the license may be particularly valuable to that licensee and thus command higher royalties. Such a license arrangement is often appropriate in the situation where a patent-holder has invented and obtained patents on certain technical innovations and now wants to capitalize on the patents, but requires a partner in order to bring a product to market that makes use of the patented innovations.

An alternate type of license is the nonexclusive license, in which the patent-holder licenses patent rights to another party, but also retains the right to license the patent rights to third parties. In addition to being the type of license that often results from a settlement with an infringer (as discussed above), a nonexclusive license is often appropriate when the patents at issue are very strong and the patented technology is very valuable. In such circumstances, it may be necessary for most or all companies that produce or sell products in the relevant technology area to obtain licenses from the patent-holder just to compete, and consequently the companies are happy to obtain a license to the patents even though their competitors may receive the same license.

Because a patent gives the patent-holder several different patent rights including the rights to exclude others from making, using and selling an invention protected by the patent, a patent-holder also has the right to exclude others from any subset of these activities and consequently has the right to license any subset of these activities. For example, the patent-holder can grant another party a license that is restricted to the *sale* of products encompassed by the patent, such that the licensee does not also have a license to make those products. Additionally, for example, the patent-holder can grant licenses that are limited in time, limited to activities within certain geographic regions, limited in terms of the specific innovations that are licensed, and limited according to a variety of other criteria.

2. Sale

Through licensing, a patent-holder can positively exercise some of the patent rights provided by a patent without completely exploiting all of those patent rights. This is analogous to the ability of an owner of real property to exploit limited rights in the property, e.g., by renting the property or by granting easements on the property. However, just as an owner of real property also has the ultimate option of completely exploiting the property rights by selling the property to another party, a patent-holder also has the option of completely exploiting all of the patent rights in a patent by selling or assigning the patent to another party.

3. Patent Rights in Finance and Marketing

In addition to being able to license or sell your patent rights, you can also use your patent rights as a basis for receiving financing from outside investors. Investors and financial experts recognize that the patents and other intellectual property of a company can constitute both a significant source of competitive advantage and a possible (if not actual) source of revenue for the company. Consequently, the patents and other intellectual property of a company can provide a justification for an increased valuation of the company, and also can serve as direct collateral via a security interest. Indeed, sometimes even potential patent rights—e.g., rights to a patent application or simply knowledge of an invention—can have significant value in this regard.

Another way of indirectly exploiting patent rights is through advertising. Advertisers have recognized that members of the public view the obtaining of a patent concerning a product as a significant indication that the product has characteristics that are desirable and constitute an improvement over other similar products. Some in the public even perceive (however incorrectly) a patent to be a "seal of approval" provided by the United States government indicating that the products encompassed by the patent are scientifically proven to be effective, safe and otherwise desirable. For these reasons, it frequently makes sense to market products as being "patented" when those products are in fact within the scope of patents. This is particularly true, for example, in the case of medications that are patented.

C. Patent Valuation

Although many patents have great value, assigning values to patents is generally a difficult task that is fraught with uncertainties and inaccuracy. Valuation experts often attempt to value patents, like many other assets, using a variety of methods. In particular, patents are frequently valued with respect to the general market for patent rights, based upon the income that the patents produce, and (less frequently) based upon the costs associated with obtaining the patents. Nevertheless, each of these bases of valuation has significant inadequacies.

1. Market Valuation

When employing market valuation, the valuer attempts to assign a value to the patent that reflects what someone else in the market for patents would pay for it. Because often the patent itself is not up for sale (and has not recently been sold), the valuer can only estimate what the market value of the patent would be based upon the values of other, similar patents that have in fact been bought or sold. Thus, the market valuation technique requires an identification of "comparables" to the patent.

Although market valuation is a useful technique in principle, market valuation of a patent is often difficult because each patent, by definition, protects a new innovation and is different from every other patent. Also, the value of a given patent depends to a large extent upon factors beyond the patent itself that are difficult to evaluate, such as the business with which the patent is or may become associated, and whether the patent is just one of a number of patents in a patent portfolio or a patent pool. Moreover, patents are not bought and sold on a very regular basis and, even when transfers of patents occur, the price information is often not readily available to outsiders. The market for patents simply is not a very liquid market. In practice, therefore, the identification of appropriate comparables in performing market valuations of patents is more difficult than the identification of appropriate comparables in valuing other types of assets such as stock.

Various parties continue to refine (or attempt to refine) market valuation techniques. For example, PLX Systems, Inc. (formerly The Patent & License Exchange) developed a database of valuations of highly focused technology companies as a source of comparables to use in its TRRU™ valuation technique. Additionally, several parties have set up (or are working on setting up) institutions that enhance the market for patent rights. For example, yet2.com (at www.yet2.com) has created an Internet-based patent "exchange," which lists patent rights that are available for sale or license, and enables those patent rights to be purchased or licensed in a standardized manner. Despite these developments, accurate market valuation continues to remain elusive.

2. Income Valuation

The purpose of income valuation is to determine the patent's worth by reference to the amount of income that the patent generates or could generate. Income valuation depends upon having information regarding past or expected income streams, and so income valuation of patents is most commonly employed with respect to patents that have already been licensed and are already commanding revenue. Also, where a company's patent rights are a significant source of competitive advantage for the company with respect to its sale of certain products or services, it may be appropriate to value those patent rights based upon the income generated by those products or services, particularly as a function of how much higher of a price the company is able to charge for those products or services as a result of the patent rights. From an income valuation perspective, a patent's value typically is affected by the amount of the patent's lifespan that is still left before the patent expires.

As with respect to the valuation of companies, a patent's income valuation can be calculated through the use of well-known valuation techniques such as the discounted cash flow technique. Relatively recently, additional sophisticated techniques such as option valuation techniques have also been applied to the valuation of patent rights, in an effort to more accurately account for some of the complexities and uncertainties associated with the exploitation of patent rights. For example, when applying option valuation methods, a patent can be viewed as an option to invest (at some time during the patent's term) capital into developing and marketing a product protected by the patent to generate income from sales of the product.

Income valuation of patents, like market valuation of patents, has serious limitations. Even when relatively clear-cut income data exists (which often is not the case), it is still difficult to capture in an income valuation all of the income contributions made by a patent. For example, even when a patent is producing a steady stream of royalties under a license agreement, the existing flow of royalty payments may not be an accurate indicator of the full licensing potential of the patent.

Further, the positive income effects that patents provide by restricting patent-holders' competitors are generally difficult to capture in income valuations. Even where a company's patent rights are clearly enhancing the company's profits with respect to the sale of certain products or services, it may nevertheless be difficult to estimate the extent to which those profits are in fact due to the patent rights. Such a determination can depend upon a variety of factors that are difficult to assess including, for example, the extent to which the particular technologies protected by the patent rights are in demand, and the ease with which competitors can design or otherwise obtain substitute technologies that circumvent the patent rights.

An additional factor that clouds the valuation (both income and market) of patents is simply the nature of patents themselves. In comparison with some other assets that are relatively clear in terms of their scope (e.g., real estate), the scope of a patent is often difficult to interpret. Not only may it be difficult to determine what the claims of a patent actually encompass, but also it may be difficult to assess the strength of the patent in terms of its assertability and ability to withstand challenges to its validity.

3. Cost Valuation

Valuing a patent according to the costs of obtaining that patent is perhaps the most straightforward way of valuing the patent, yet it is rarely sufficient as a method of patent valuation. Unlike some other assets that have market, income and cost valuations that are closely aligned due to market forces and due to the predictability of costs and benefits associated with creating and exploiting those assets, a patent's cost valuation often has no relationship to its market or income valuations. Indeed, it is not uncommon for a U.S. patent to cost well under $20,000 to obtain and at the same time produce hundreds of thousands of dollars (or, in the case of a drug patent, millions of dollars) in royalty income. Even if one views technology development costs as part of the costs of obtaining patent rights, the cost valuation of a patent often will be less than its market or income valuations.

4. What Is a Patent Really Worth?

From the above, it should be clear that the various techniques for valuing patents can produce widely varying valuations of the same patent. Indeed, the process of valuing patents is sufficiently obscure that, in many circumstances, parties give up on attempting to accurately calculate patents' value but instead resort to simple (and largely imprecise) proxies for that value. For example, during cross-licensing negotiations involving many patents, parties sometimes merely count up the number of patents of each of the respective parties and simply use the number of patents of each party as a proxy for the relative value of the party's respective patent rights. Further, to the extent that the respective parties have similarly large numbers of patents, the parties may ascribe equal values to one another's patents even though the numbers of patents of the parties are not exactly identical.

While the various valuation techniques seldom produce identical results, it is important to note that each of the various valuation techniques does have its own particular merits in specific situations. For example, the market valuation technique is a more accurate technique than the other two techniques when there are very close and obvious comparables for the patent being valued. The income valuation technique is more accurate when clear licensing agreements are already in place, and where those licensing agreements represent the primary way in which the patent rights are being exploited. The cost valuation technique is only appropriate in rare situations such as, for example, when calculating a patent's value for tax write-off purposes.

D. Portfolio Strategy

If one patent is valuable, a portfolio of patents can be even more so. Indeed, a portfolio of patents can magnify the values of the individual patents within the portfolio and thus can be worth more than the sum of its parts. A patent portfolio can enhance the value of the patents within the portfolio both in terms of the competitive advantage that the patents provide, and in terms of the value of the patents as marketable assets.

1. Enhancement of Competitive Advantage

From the standpoint of competitive advantage, a portfolio of several patents in the same technology area can operate as a series of roadblocks or as a minefield. As the number of patents in the portfolio increases, it may become more and more difficult for competitors to design around or otherwise avoid the patents in an efficient manner. Not only may an increased number of patents in fact encompass a larger proportion of a technology area, but also the costs involved in determining the scope of the patents at issue can become prohibitive. Further, the existence of a large patent portfolio can be intimidating in that it suggests that the patent-holder may be more vigilant in monitoring for others' use of the patented technology, and may have exercised greater care in pursuing strong patent rights.

When infringement does occur, a portfolio of patents increases the patent-holder's ability to assert the patents, especially when multiple patents of the portfolio are being infringed. While the chance that any given patent is invalid may be a particular percentage, the chance that multiple patents simultaneously being asserted are all invalid is significantly less. Having a portfolio of patents also can be particularly valuable when negotiating cross-licensing arrangements with other parties that similarly have portfolios of patents.

2. Enhancement of Patents As a Product

The value-enhancing effects of a patent portfolio also exist for a company that desires to license or sell its patent rights. When well-developed, a patent portfolio encompasses multiple portions of a technology area in order to increase the difficulty of designing around the patents of the portfolio. Yet, a patent portfolio need not encompass all portions of a technology area in order to enhance the value of the patents in the portfolio. In some technology areas, certain technical features are interrelated with other technical features to a sufficient extent that it is not practical to use some of the features without the others. In such technology areas, a patent portfolio can attain significant value once it "covers enough of the bases," that is, encompasses enough of the different interrelated technical features so that most would-be users of the technology must at least use something that is encompassed by one or more of the patents of the portfolio.

Additionally, once a portfolio of patents encompasses a critical proportion of an overall technology area, the owner of that portfolio begins to appear to its competitors and others as a major player in that technology area. This perception can strengthen the patent-holder's position as it attempts to negotiate licenses of its patent rights with others. Indeed, some potential licensees may find it desirable to license patent rights from the holder of a patent portfolio simply as a way of maintaining good relations with the patent-holder so that the patent-holder may be inclined to license additional technologies to the licensees in the future.

3. Filling in the Gaps

Rarely is it possible for a patent-holder to develop patent rights that completely encompass an entire technology area. Usually, this only occurs when entirely new technologies or technology standards are emerging, and the patent-holder is the key developer of the new technologies or proponent of the new technology standards. Much more typically, it is the case that a patent-holder's competitors have already developed certain aspects of a technology, and consequently the patent-holder is only able to obtain patent rights encompassing somewhat different aspects of the technology and "fill in the gaps" of the technology area.

Though limited, a portfolio with such scope is often sufficient to establish the patent-holder as a significant player in the technology area. What is important for a patent-holder is not so much that the patent-holder obtain patent rights encompassing all of a technology area, but rather that the patent-holder identify segments of the technology area that are potentially valuable in the marketplace and available for protection by the patent-holder's patent rights, and to obtain as many patent rights concerning these segments of the technology area as possible.

4. Dominant and Subordinate Patents

Suppose that one patent covers all vehicles having four doors and two headlights, and another patent covers all vehicles having four doors, two headlights and a radio. In such case, the second patent is entirely dominated by (and subordinate to) the first patent, in the sense that the first patent also covers all vehicles covered by the second patent. Thus, in the absence of a license with respect to the first patent, the holder of the second patent could not sell vehicles covered by the second patent without infringing the first patent (in contrast, the holder of the first patent merely might not be able to sell a car with a radio).

Also, for example, suppose that a first patent covers all vehicles having four wheels and two headlights, while a second patent covers all vehicles having four doors and two headlights. In such case, the coverage of the first patent overlaps to some extent the coverage of the second patent, since both patents cover vehicles having four wheels, two headlights and four doors. At the same time, neither of the patents fully dominates, or is subordinate to, the other. For example, while it would be possible for the first patent to cover a car with two doors that is not covered by the second patent, it would also be possible for the second patent to cover a vehicle with only three wheels that is not covered by the first patent. Further, although neither patent fully dominates the other, each of the patents nevertheless partly dominates the other with respect to a particular aspect of technology. That is, from the standpoint of four-wheel vehicles, the first patent dominates the second patent and, from the standpoint of four-door vehicles, the second patent dominates the first patent.

These examples demonstrate that patents can dominate other patents, partially or totally. While being subordinate to another patent may sometimes reduce the subordinate patent's value, this is not necessarily so and, in any event, a subordinate patent certainly is capable of having significant value. Indeed, while patents having broader scope generally are more valuable than patents having narrower scope, patents protecting new innovations concerning specialized implementations of an older, broader technology may nevertheless have more value than the patents concerning the older technology.

These relationships among patents involving the domination of one patent by another can be of importance to parties as they develop their patent portfolios. For example, a company can strengthen its patent portfolio by focusing its innovations and patent portfolio development on segments of a technology area that are likely to become critical segments or "bottlenecks" of the technology area, and by focusing on obtaining patents that will likely dominate the future patents of others. Also for example, a patent-holder may effectively extend the term of the patent-holder's older patents by obtaining additional patents protecting new and preferred embodiments of the technology of the older patents.

5. Claim Diversification

Regardless of how well a party is able to determine the likely ways in which a technology area will develop, the party may want to diversify its patent portfolio by obtaining patent coverage along different dimensions of the technology area. The diversification could occur not only in terms of particular technical features, but also in terms of how the technical innovations will eventually be made, used or sold. For example, patent coverage often can be obtained both with respect to the structures associated with a given technology and with respect to the methods of operation associated with that technology, by using different types of claims, e.g., by using both apparatus claims and method claims. Further, patent coverage can be obtained both with respect to entire technical systems and with respect to subcomponents within those systems, such as aftermarket or replacement parts.

E. Patents in Comparison With Other Types of Intellectual Property

While the patent rights afforded by patents constitute some of the "intellectual property" rights that can be obtained with respect to ideas and other similar intangibles, copyrights, trademarks, trade secrets and other types of intellectual property assets also provide intellectual property rights. These non-patent intellectual property assets each have their own characteristics and serve their own particular purposes, which differ from those of patents. It is worthwhile understanding, at least to some extent, how these different intellectual property assets compare to patents so that one can determine what types of intellectual property assets are appropriate to obtain in a given circumstance.

1. Patents in Comparison With Trade Secrets

A trade secret is a type of intellectual property asset that arises when secret information is developed and efforts are made to prevent the revelation of that secret information to outsiders. Trade secret rights mainly include rights to sue those who have stolen or otherwise improperly made use of the secrets. In contrast to patent rights, which are granted by federal law, state law typically confers trade secret rights.

As discussed above, patents serve the purpose of encouraging public disclosure and are granted in exchange for the public disclosure of inventions by their inventors. Consequently, once a patent issues, its content cannot be a trade secret. In contrast, trade secrets merely serve the purpose of protecting individuals and companies from inappropriate espionage. While a trade secret expires when the secret information is made public, it may last perpetually if the information does not become public. A trade secret is not infringed when others independently develop the secret information, while a patent can still be infringed by others who have independently developed the patented invention.

2. Patents in Comparison With Copyrights

While utility patents protect the substance of useful, inventive ideas, copyrights protect the forms in which ideas are expressed. Therefore, while a person is not free to make, use or sell articles that employ the ideas claimed in another's unexpired patent, one is free to copy the ideas in a copyrighted work as long as one does not substantially copy the form in which those ideas are expressed, and one does not violate a copyright if one independently came up with the copyrighted work. Copyrights and patents also have different life spans. While a utility patent typically only lasts about 20 years from its earliest filing date, a copyright lasts considerably longer (e.g., 70 years beyond the life of the author of the copyrighted work with respect to certain works, 95 or 120 years with respect to other works).

While computer software may constitute a patentable invention, computer software also normally consists of programming code that is a copyrightable work. Indeed, for many years, computer programmers and software companies preferred to obtain protection for their computer software by way of copyrights (and sometimes trade secrets) rather than patents because of the relative inexpensiveness and ease of obtaining copyrights and because, up until only recently, there was a lack of clarity in the patent law as to the extent to which computer software inventions could be patented.

3. Patents in Comparison With Source Designation Assets

Trademarks, service marks, certification marks, trade names, trade dress and similar intangible assets protect indications of the source of a product or service. Although commonly grouped along with patents and copyrights into the category of "intellectual property," these assets are substantially different from patents and copyrights. While patents and copyrights are designed to protect new creative ideas and expressions, source designation assets are protective of concepts such as names and symbols that are often neither particularly new nor particularly creative. Source designation assets also differ from patents and copyrights, which have fixed life spans, in that the rights associated with these assets such as trademark rights (and even registrations for trademarks) potentially can last forever. Many source designation assets can be protected by way of both federal and state laws.

Despite the differences between patents and source designation assets, there is one circumstance in which the two types of intellectual property may overlap. Specifically, when a product has design features that have a functional aspect, but are not primarily dictated by function, the features potentially can be protected by way of both patent and trade dress rights.

4. Other Forms of Intellectual Property

A variety of other types of intellectual property assets exist as well. These include, for example, mask works rights that can be obtained to protect the masks used to create semiconductor chips, and contractual intellectual property assets such as confidentiality agreements used to protect the confidential information of a company.

CHAPTER **3**

What Is Patentable?

The patent law defines what a patentable invention is—that is, the patent law defines the conditions that must be met in order for an innovation to be patented. The following is a summary of how the patent law defines a patentable invention, particularly with respect to inventions relating to computer software, business methods and the Internet.

A. The Definition of a Patentable Invention

The definition of a patentable invention set forth in the patent law is a definition that takes into account the purposes of the patent system, and is somewhat different from what some may consider to be a more common sense definition of an invention. As a result, not all innovations that one might intuitively consider to be inventive can be patented, and some innovations or ideas that one might consider to be hardly or not at all inventive can nevertheless still be patented.

Whether an invention as claimed in a patent application (or patent) is patentable generally depends upon whether the invention is of a specified subject matter, whether the invention is useful, whether the invention is novel, and whether the invention is nonobvious. The determination of whether the invention in a patent application is patentable can vary from claim to claim. That is, even if the invention as recited in one claim or set of claims is determined to be not patentable, it is still possible for the invention as recited in other claims of the patent application to be patentable.

1. Patentable Subject Matter

First, to be patentable, a claimed invention must generally belong to one of the different "types" of patentable subject matter that are identified in the patent statutes. These include processes, machines, manufactures, and compositions of matter (and improvements thereof). For example, courts have recently confirmed that Internet-related and business method innovations can fit within these categories of patentable subject matter, and courts have for some time held that software can be patentable (at least when associated with a concrete industrial result).

2. Utility

The patent law also requires that, to be patentable, the claimed invention must have practical utility (usefulness) beyond the trivial. The question of whether an invention has sufficient utility tends to be of significance primarily with respect to inventions in certain areas of technology such as biochemistry, chemistry and pharmaceuticals where a composition may be novel but its use may still be undiscovered or unproven. Thus, for example, it may be necessary that a chemical have a meaningful utility as a cleanser, rather than simply a trivial utility as filler for a paperweight, in order for the chemical to be patented. In contrast, with respect to inventions in the mechanical and electrical arts, the issue of whether the inventions have sufficient utility seldom arises.

3. Novelty and Prior Art

Novelty is also required for an invention to be patentable. The novelty or newness of a claimed invention depends upon a comparison of that invention with what is already deemed to exist, that is, with the "prior art." Specifically, if any single prior art informational source or reference shows (or inherently teaches) all of the limitations of a given claim concerning an invention, then that claim is invalid for a lack of novelty. Conversely, if no single prior art reference shows every one of the limitations of a given claim, then the invention as recited in that claim is novel.

This definition of novelty, of course, begs the question as to what can actually constitute prior art. Determining what constitutes prior art under the U.S. patent law is complicated. The complexity largely is due to the fact that the U.S. patent law attempts to meet multiple goals in defining what can be novel. For example, while one goal of the U.S. patent law is to avoid giving patent protection to ideas that are already available to the public, another goal is to encourage inventors to submit patent applications concerning their inventions to the Patent Office without unwarranted delay to promote the rapid public disclosure of those inventions, and a further goal is to give inventors enough time to develop their inventions (and evaluate their commercial potential) before submitting patent applications. In attempting to achieve and balance these various goals, the U.S. patent law provides a variety of rules regarding when something can be considered prior art.

a. Prior Art Arising Because of Prior Invention by Another

One type of prior art against which your invention may be compared in order to determine its novelty is prior art indicating that your invention already existed and was available to the public when you came up with the invention. In particular, this type of prior art includes information showing that your invention was known or used by others in the United States, or patented or described in a printed publication in any country, before the time at which you invented your invention. To qualify as being known or used, the invention must have been known or used in a public, rather than secretive, manner.

Additionally, the patent law provides that a published U.S. patent application constitutes prior art with respect to your invention if another party filed the patent application before you came up with your invention. Similarly, an issued patent constitutes prior art if another party filed the patent application upon which the patent was granted before you came up with your invention. Further, PCT patent application publications under some circumstances also can constitute prior art as of their filing date.

b. Statutory Drop-Dead Bar Dates

The patent law also provides that you cannot obtain a patent if your invention was patented or described in a printed publication in any country, or in public use or on sale in the United States, more than one year prior to the date on which you first file a patent application regarding your invention. Thus, the prior art includes all patents and printed publications relating to your invention that were issued or published more than one year prior to your earliest filing date. Further, the prior art includes information showing that anyone publicly used or sold the invention in the United States more than one year prior to your earliest filing date. The courts have determined that even offering an invention for sale can constitute "selling" of the invention.[1]

By defining the prior art to include these types of art, the patent law provides an incentive to inventors to promptly file their patent applications, and eventually provide public disclosure of their inventions. References or other information falling into these categories effectively create one-year "drop-dead" bar dates by which any U.S. patent application on the invention must be filed. For example, if an article disclosing your invention was published on January 1st of the current year, you have up until the end of January 1st of the coming new year to file a U.S. patent application on your invention (even though January 1st is a holiday). This incentive to speed up the filing of your patent application generally exists even when you are not aware of any specific references that have created drop-dead bar dates since, by delaying the filing of your patent application, you risk exposing your patent application to more and more prior art references.

It is important that inventors be aware of these prior art provisions of the patent law, since patent rights cannot be recovered once they have been lost due to a failure to file a patent application by a drop-dead bar date. These provisions of the patent law are particularly perilous for an inventor because the inventor himself or herself may create a bar date. For example, if you invent something and you publish an article on your invention (or offer it for sale at a trade show), you yourself will have created a one-year bar date that will preclude you from obtaining a patent unless you file your patent application within the one-year grace period afforded by the patent law.

---

1. Additionally, another provision of the patent law prevents you from obtaining a U.S. patent on your invention if you did not file your patent application in the United States until after a foreign patent (or "inventor's certificate") was issued on your invention, if the foreign patent issued from a patent application that you had filed more than one year prior to the date on which you filed your patent application in the United States.

c. Priority

An additional provision of the patent law provides that you are precluded from obtaining a patent if it is shown that, before you came up with your invention, your invention was made in this country by another inventor who had not abandoned, suppressed or concealed the invention. The provision goes on to state that the considerations to be evaluated in determining priority of invention will include not only the respective dates of conception and reduction to practice, but also the reasonable diligence of one who was the first to conceive and the last to reduce to practice from a time prior to conception by the other.[2]

Consequently, while the patent law of the United States is generally oriented towards awarding a patent to the first inventor of a given invention (and specifically forbids the awarding of a patent to someone who did not make the invention), it is not always the first inventor of an invention that is granted a patent on the invention. In particular, even if you are the first inventor of an invention, you can still lose your ability to obtain a patent on your invention to another person if you abandon, suppress or conceal your invention between the time at which you conceived your invention and a later time at which you begin serious, continuing efforts to "reduce your invention to practice."[3]

d. Absolute Novelty Bars

While the one-year drop-dead bar dates in the United States may seem draconian, the laws of most foreign countries are much less forgiving. In particular, most foreign countries have "absolute novelty" laws that preclude an inventor from obtaining a patent on his or her invention if the inventor has not yet filed a patent application somewhere on the invention by the time at which that invention is first publicly disclosed in any form. That is, rather than providing an inventor with a one-year grace period within which to file a patent application after a public

---

2. A similar provision also applies to "interference proceedings," which occur when multiple patent applications claiming the same invention are copending before the Patent Office or when a patent application is pending before the Patent Office that claims the same invention as one or more unexpired patents. In such proceedings, the Patent Office determines which of the patent application(s) or patent(s) has priority and may determine which of the patent claims are patentable.

3. An invention is finally "reduced to practice" either when it has been successfully implemented and tested, or when a patent application concerning the invention has been filed.

disclosure, these foreign countries immediately deprive an inventor of his or her patent rights once disclosure occurs prior to the filing of a patent application.

4. Nonobviousness

The patent statutes further require that, to be patentable, a claimed invention must not have been obvious at the time the invention was made to a person having ordinary skill in the art relating to the invention, in view of the prior art. This is the "nonobviousness" requirement of patentability.

Most references that would be prior art in determining whether an invention is novel are also prior art in determining whether the invention is nonobvious. However, certain subject matter that constitutes prior art in determining the novelty of an invention does not constitute prior art in determining the invention's nonobviousness, so long as that subject matter and the invention were commonly owned by, or under an obligation of assignment to, the same party at the time the invention was made. That is, your invention may be shielded from being found obvious in view of certain types of subject matter that were created by others within your organization (e.g., your work colleagues), albeit in some cases it may still be necessary to take steps to avoid "double-patenting" rejections in view of such subject matter as discussed further below.

Each of the limitations in a claim must still be considered in determining whether the claim is obvious. However, while a claim concerning an invention is shown to lack novelty only if one can find a single prior art reference that expressly or inherently shows every limitation of the claim, the claim can be shown to be obvious if a combination of multiple prior art references shows every limitation and if it would have been obvious to a person of ordinary skill in the art pertaining to the invention to combine those references to arrive at the invention. Further, a claim can be shown to be obvious if it would have been obvious to a person of ordinary skill in the art pertaining to the invention to modify the prior art to arrive at the invention, despite the fact that certain claim limitations are not explicitly or inherently disclosed in the prior art.

Given the statutory definition of nonobviousness, determining whether an invention is nonobvious requires a determination of what a fictitious person of "ordinary skill in the art" relating to the invention would have known. Of course, a real person of ordinary skill in the art would not have known of all possibly relevant prior art in all areas of technology. Nevertheless, in the context of a nonobviousness determination, the patent law presumes that a fictitious person of ordinary skill in the art would have known about key art, that is, prior art pertaining to the particular technology area in question and analogous areas of technology. Further, the patent case law has specified a number of specific criteria that normally should be considered in determining the level of ordinary skill in the art. These criteria include, for example, the types of problems encountered in the art, the solutions to those problems found in the prior art, the level of sophistication in the technology, and the typical educational levels of persons working in the art.

Once a determination has been made as to the scope of prior art that would have been available to a person of ordinary skill in the art, it is possible to ascertain the differences between a claimed invention and that prior art. Although it is possible for a claimed invention to be found obvious in view of a combination of prior art references or in view of one or more references when appropriately modified, the patent law places restrictions upon whether any given combination or modification is allowable for this purpose. In particular, the patent law provides that, for a claim concerning an invention to be obvious in view of several prior art references, where each of the references shows only some of the limitations of the claim, there must be a teaching or suggestion arising from the prior art (at least implicitly or generally in view of the level of ordinary skill in the art or the type of problem being addressed) that would have motivated a person of ordinary skill in the art to combine those references. Similarly, for a claim to be an obvious modification of something shown in the prior art, there must be a teaching or suggestion arising from the prior art that would have motivated a person of ordinary skill in the art to make the modification. Thus, according to the patent law, a person of ordinary skill in the art would only have known to combine or modify prior art references to achieve a particular result if the prior art also provided a suggestion to make that combination or modification.

In addition to the above considerations, the patent case law also has enumerated certain "secondary considerations" or types of evidence that can be provided that are at least somewhat indicative of nonobviousness. These secondary considerations include, for example, whether there has been a long felt but unsatisfied need, a failure in the past to solve the problem solved by the invention, and/or commercial success of the invention that clearly stems from the invention itself. Other secondary considerations include whether competitors have directly copied the claimed invention, whether the technology has been licensed by others in industry, whether persons skilled in the art of the invention have tended to teach away from the invention, and whether the results of the invention were unexpected to those skilled in the art of the invention. Whether a claimed invention is obvious thus often turns on a variety of types of factual evidence.

5. Double Patenting

It is only possible for an inventor to obtain a single patent on an invention. Consequently, if the invention claimed in your patent application is identical to that recited by claim(s) in another patent of yours, the patent application will be rejected for double patenting.

Further, if the invention claimed in your application is an obvious variation of that recited by claim(s) in another patent of yours, the patent application also will be rejected, albeit such a rejection can often be overcome by giving up a portion of the term of any patent issuing from the pending application so that the patent is in force no longer than the other patent that was the basis of the double-patenting rejection. These prohibitions on double patenting are equally applicable where the pending application and the patent on which the rejection is based are commonly assigned to the same company.

B. Computer Software, Internet-Related Innovations, and Business Methods as Patentable Subject Matter

At the turn of the millennium, there was an explosion of inventions in areas such as computer software, the Internet, business methods and biotechnology. Attempts to patent some of these inventions, particularly in the areas of computer software, the Internet and business methods, challenged previously held notions of what is patentable. Recent court decisions now provide a solid basis for believing that the patent laws broadly extend patent protection to inventions in these areas.

1. Modern Case Law Concerning Computer-Related Inventions and Reactions by Congress and the Patent Office

Over the past 20 years, the patent law has responded dramatically to the rapid development and growth in the use of computers, and in particular to the explosion in the number of computer software inventions. Early on in this development, the simplest of these computer software inventions were looked upon as mere mathematical ideas ("algorithms") that were outside the bounds of patentable subject matter. Because computer software fundamentally involves a set of computer instructions expressible as program code, computer software inventions were for a time looked upon as something better protected by the copyright laws than by the patent laws.

Yet, it is often difficult to obtain broad protection over the functions of computer software inventions by way of the copyright laws. The copyright laws are intended to protect specific forms of a created work rather than to prevent the unauthorized use of underlying ideas. Because it is often possible to write a program that performs substantially the same functions as a copyrighted computer program even though the two programs are substantially different in their particular program instructions, it is often possible to employ the basic ideas of an inventive computer program while skirting the copyright protection of that computer program. Given these limitations associated with attempting to protect computer software inventions by way of the copyright laws, significant economic pressure arose to modify the patent laws so that computer software inventions could more clearly fall within the bounds of what is patentable subject matter.

a. State Street Bank

The watershed case in the development of the patent law toward a more expansive view of patent protection for computer software inventions was *State Street Bank & Trust Co. v. Signature Financial Group Inc.*, 149 F.3d 1368, 47 USPQ2d 1596 (Fed. Cir. 1998). In *State Street Bank*, the Federal Circuit articulated at least two important holdings concerning whether computer-related inventions can be patentable subject matter.

First, the Federal Circuit clarified its interpretation of past cases involving inventions making use of mathematical algorithms. While not disputing that a simple mathematical formula, without more, cannot be patented, the Federal Circuit stated that the practical application of a mathematical formula to produce a "useful, concrete and tangible result" can be patented. Thus, there is nothing significant restricting a computer program invention that is employed to produce a useful, concrete and tangible result from being patented so long as it meets the normal criteria for patentability—that is, so long as the invention concerns patentable subject matter, and the invention is useful, novel and nonobvious.

Second, the Federal Circuit also did away with the so-called "business method" exception to patentability. According to this doctrine, inventions having to do with business plans, strategies and systems (e.g., a red tag sale at an appliance store) were argued by some to be outside the realm of patentable subject matter. Yet in *State Street Bank*, the Federal Circuit held that inventions relating to business methods are no less patentable than any other types of inventions. So long as an invention relating to a business method meets the normal criteria for patentability, the invention can be patented.

b. Reactions to State Street Bank

These developments in the patent law concerning computer-related inventions, as well as the development of the Internet and e-commerce, have had significant effects upon the numbers and types of patent applications that are being filed in the Patent Office. In recent years, the number of filed patent applications concerning computer software-related inventions, and especially those inventions relating to the Internet and e-commerce, have soared. For example, the number of patent applications classified as computer-related business method patent applications (Patent Office class 705) grew from about 1,340 in 1998 to about 8,200 in 2001. Some examples of patents that have issued in these areas are described below.

The issuance of certain business method patents, particularly patents such as the so-called "one-click" patent (U.S. Patent No. 5,960,411) assigned to Amazon.com, Inc., has prompted criticism from certain segments of the public who consider these patents to be improperly protective of arguably obvious subject matter. Although some of the furor surrounding these patents is unjustified—largely because of off-the-cuff, overly broad interpretations of what these patents actually cover—some of the concerns are justified. In particular, because the

Internet and other technologies relating to business method patent applications were and are developing at a rapid pace, and because much of the prior art concerning these technology areas can be difficult to find, there is reasonable cause for concern that the Patent Office may not be adequately able to identify relevant prior art in conducting its examination of these patent applications.

c. Response by Congress in AIPA

The growing concern surrounding business method patents, especially following the *State Street Bank* case, was one of the considerations that led Congress to pass the American Inventors Protection Act in 1999. Among its various provisions, AIPA included several provisions intended to address concerns relating to business method patents.

One of these provisions set forth by AIPA is the first inventor's defense, which was created to address the concerns of businesses that, after developing and secretly using their own Internet-related business methods for some time, have been shocked to learn that others are able to obtain patents covering those very same business methods. In accordance with the first inventor's defense, if an inventor has invented something relating to "business methods," the inventor had the invention at least one year before a competitor's patent application concerning the same invention was filed in the Patent Office, and the inventor commercially used the invention before the competitor's patent application was filed, then the inventor has a defense to charges of infringement asserted by the competitor (even if the inventor never made the invention public).

Other provisions of AIPA cause patent applications to be published 18 months after the applications are filed unless the parties filing the patent applications specifically indicate that they do not intend to file any foreign patent applications concerning the same inventions. These provisions are similar to the practices of other countries, which routinely publish patent applications. Additionally, U.S. patent application publications now constitute prior art as of the filing dates of the patent applications. Because technologies being developed and patented are disclosed to the public by way of patent application publications earlier than would otherwise be the case, the Patent Office has an easier time identifying prior art that is relevant to other patent applications (e.g., applications relating to business method inventions) undergoing prosecution.

Because it may often take two or more years for a patent application to issue as a patent, the publication rules create a situation in which an inventor's competitors may learn of the inventor's technologies before the inventor can protect those technologies with a patent. In an attempt to offset these possible disadvantages associated with publication, AIPA also creates "provisional rights," whereby an inventor can sometimes recoup royalties for others' use of the inventor's invention between the time of publication of the inventor's patent application and the time at which the patent application eventually issues as a patent. However, these provisional rights may often be difficult to enforce and, indeed, may never materialize at all if the differences between the claims published in the patent application publication and the claims that eventually issue in the patent are significant.

Consequently, despite the existence of provisional rights, patent application publication should give pause to some inventors, particularly those innovating in rapidly developing technical areas such as computer software and the Internet, whose inventions may be most valuable within the first few years after being conceived. These inventors should determine, prior to filing their U.S. patent applications, whether they intend to file foreign patent applications. If not, the inventors should consider whether early publication of their patent applications would be detrimental and, if so, they should consider asserting their intention not to file foreign patent applications to the Patent Office to avoid early publication.

d. Response by the Patent Office

The Patent Office also responded to the *State Street Bank* case and the growing concern surrounding business method patents by clarifying the manner in which it examines computer-related inventions and by heightening the scrutiny with which it examines business method patents.

In particular, the MPEP (Manual of Patent Examining Procedure) of the Patent Office now provides explicitly that the patentability of computer-related inventions should be determined under the "useful, concrete and tangible result" standard of *State Street Bank* rather than previous standards. The MPEP further provides that, when considering computer-related patent applications, the Patent Office should verify that there is a practical, functional aspect to the inventions. While "functional, descriptive" material standing alone, e.g., computer program code or data structures without any accompanying computer hardware, may not be patentable since the material cannot function by itself, the existence of this material in a computer memory device may be a patentable invention since the material can become functional by way of the memory device.

The MPEP also enumerates certain types of computer-related inventions that are likely to constitute patentable subject matter. A process may meet the test of patentable subject matter if it includes at least some action(s) to be performed outside of the computer that result in a physical transformation. Also, processes that involve taking measurements of physical objects or actions and then manipulating that data into computer data may be considered patentable subject matter. Of course, even though a particular invention is considered to be patentable subject matter, the invention still must meet the other tests of patentability (utility, novelty and nonobviousness) in order to be patentable.

The Patent Office also has worked hard at developing more up-to-date databases and other resources that Patent Examiners can search in order to identify prior art relating to patent applications concerning business method inventions, and has stepped up its requirements that Patent Examiners actually conduct searches using these tools. Additionally, the Patent Office now requires that, whenever a Patent Examiner determines that such a patent application is allowable to issue as a patent, a supervising Patent Examiner must review this determination. It appears that the implementation of these procedures has significantly slowed down the issuance of patent applications relating to business methods, arguably to an excessive extent.

e. Trends in Business Method Patents

Despite these responses by Congress and by the Patent Office to the concerns surrounding computer-related inventions, particularly those relating to the Internet and business methods, some persons believe that still further restrictions should be placed upon business method patents. For example, in 2000, a bill was proposed to Congress that would have created additional, special ways for third parties to challenge business method patent applications and patents, and that would have changed the standard of proof required to be met by would-be challengers of business method patents.

Nevertheless, it appears rather unlikely that further stringent rules will be legislated by Congress restricting business method or other computer-related patents. It particularly appears unlikely that either the courts or Congress will roll back the *State Street Bank* decision in favor of a more restrictive view of what types of computer-related inventions should be patentable. From a philosophical standpoint, there does not appear to be any good reason why computer-related inventions that meet the normal criteria of patentability should be any less patentable than any other type of invention. The rationale for providing patent protection is just as applicable with regard to computer-related inventions as with regard to any other type of invention.

Significant new restrictions on computer-related inventions also appear unlikely from a practical standpoint. Not only has some of the economic pressure for such legislation disappeared with the bursting of the "Internet bubble" in 2000 and 2001, but also there are increasing indications that the changes already implemented by Congress and the Patent Office are addressing the concern that invalid business method patents not be issued by the Patent Office. In particular, while the number of business method patent applications (in Patent Office class 705) continued to increase from 2000 to 2001 from about 7,800 patent applications to about 8,200 patent applications, the number of business method patents issued by the Patent Office declined significantly between 2000 and 2001, from about 700 patents to about 400 patents. Although some of the decrease may be the result of the slowing down of the prosecution of these patent applications, at least some of the decrease can probably be attributed to an increasing number of rejections by the Patent Office.

2. Examples of Patents Relating to Computer Software, the Internet/E-commerce, and Business Methods

Thousands of patents are now being issued yearly by the Patent Office in the areas of computer software, the Internet/e-commerce and business methods. The following discussion concerns some examples of recently issued patents in these areas. The patents illustrate that, while often interrelated with the Internet and e-commerce, computer software innovations and business method innovations need not always involve the Internet/e-commerce. Indeed, while the Patent Office groups computer-related business method patent applications into a single class 705, there are numerous other classes into which patent applications concerning computer software and business methods can fall.

a. Computer Software Patents

Two examples of recent computer software-related patents are U.S. Patent Nos. 6,272,074 ("the '074 patent") and 6,324,546 ("the '546 patent), copies of which can be viewed and obtained by visiting the U.S. Patent and Trademark Office website (at www.uspto.gov). Both of these patents were issued in the latter half of 2001, and the '074 patent and the '546 patent were originally assigned to Oracle Corporation and Microsoft Corporation, respectively.

The titles and abstracts found on the cover pages of the '074 patent and the '546 patent are indicative of the general subject matter of those patents. The '074 patent is for a method and apparatus for generating recurring events in an electronic calendar/schedule system, while the '546 patent relates to an operating system that logs information regarding the usage of application programs in a computer so that it is possible to determine which applications are being most frequently used. In addition to providing the titles and abstracts of the patents, the cover pages of the patents additionally identify the patents' inventors and assignees, the Patent Office classifications of the patents, the issue dates of the patents, the filing dates of the corresponding patent applications, references that were cited during prosecution of the patent applications, and drawings representative of significant aspects of the patented inventions. The cover page of the '074 patent further indicates that the application corresponding to that patent actually was a continuation of two prior applications.

Following the cover pages are the figures/drawings of the patents, which in turn are followed by the specifications of the patents (aside from the abstracts/titles) including the claims sections at the ends of the patents. Of particular interest in the specifications of the '074 and '546 patents is the relative lack of disclosure of specific programming code. Rather than providing program instructions, the '074 patent primarily discloses the inventive programming in the form of flow diagrams in Figs. 1A–1E, which are discussed in columns seven through nine of the patent specification. The '546 patent provides a flow chart (e.g., at Fig. 2A) as well as shows data structures (e.g., at Figs. 2B and 2C), but in the way of programming code only provides a minimal amount of pseudo code statements (e.g., at column eight, lines 13–22 of the specification). Thus, the '074 and '546 patents illustrate that higher-level descriptions often are sufficient to enable computer-related inventions and to describe the best modes of these inventions.

Turning to the claims sections at the ends of the '074 and '546 patents, several of the claims of these patents are quite short and provide relatively broad coverage, with the broadest claims being the independent claims (for example, claims 1, 6 and 9 of the '546 patent). Also, the claims of the '074 and '546 patents exemplify several of the more commonly employed formats for claiming computer-related inventions. Each of the patents includes method claims, in which the computer software-related inventions are claimed as series of steps that are performed (see, for example, claim 1 of each patent). Each of the patents also includes general system or apparatus claims in which the inventions are claimed as computer systems or portions thereof (see, for example, claim 20 of each patent).

Additionally, the patents also include means-plus-function type claims in which the inventions are claimed as means for performing certain specified functions (see, for example, claim 15 of the '074 patent and claim 18 of the '546 patent). Also, the patents each claim their computer software-related inventions in a format in which the inventions are recited as computer-readable storage media in which specified computer instructions for performing certain functions are stored (see, for example, claim 16 of the '074 patent and claim 6 of the '546 patent). Further, the '546 patent also claims the invention in the form of an operating system having various modules (for example, see claim 9).

b. Business Method Patents

Also shown in Appendix A are two examples of patents relating to business methods. U.S. Patent No. 5,193,056 ("the '056 patent"), a copy of which can be obtained at the Patent Office website, is the business method patent that was the subject of the seminal *State Street Bank* case discussed above and, as such, is in some sense the archetypal business method patent. As is evident from the title and abstract of that patent, the invention in the patent is a data processing system for monitoring, recording and calculating information as necessary to maintain a "Hub and Spoke" financial services configuration. Claim 1 of the patent recites the invention in means-plus-function format, specifically as a data processing system having means for performing various data processing functions concerning assets in a portfolio.

Although the '056 patent generally relates to a business method, the patent nevertheless primarily concerns a data processing system and so in large part is a computer hardware and software-related patent rather than strictly a business method patent. Yet the Patent Office also allows the patenting of inventions that involve little or no machinery (computers or otherwise) and instead are largely, if not entirely, business methods or other processes performed by human actors. One such patent is U.S. Patent No. 5,851,117 ("the '117 patent"), which concerns a system and method for training cleaning personnel (also available at the Patent Office website). As shown in the figures of that patent, the invention primarily concerns a set of actions that a human trainer is to take in instructing a cleaning person on how to perform his or her cleaning job. The actions include the use of various charts that have been created showing important aspects of the cleaning jobs. Claim 1 of the patent specifically claims the invention as a method that primarily involves steps to be performed by a human trainer, such as telling a cleaning person about certain procedures to be performed and then showing physically the cleaning person how to perform those procedures. The only technical aids that form part of the claimed invention are documents that illustrate aspects of the cleaning procedures to be performed.

c. Internet/E-commerce Patents

Patents relating to the Internet and e-commerce frequently concern innovations that implement computer-related technologies to perform various business methods. Two patents that exemplify these characteristics (copies of which also can be obtained at the Patent Office website) are U.S. Patent No. 5,797,127 ("the '127 patent"), which was assigned to Walker Asset Management Limited Partnership (the parent of Priceline.com), and U.S. Patent No. 6,302,698 ("the '698 patent"). The '127 patent in particular concerns a method, apparatus and program for determining prices for options to purchase airline tickets, and then facilitating the sale or exercise of those options, while the '698 patent relates to a system for allowing online teaching.

The computer-related technologies that are discussed and claimed in e-commerce–type patents often involve Internet technologies such as web servers, websites, browser-equipped remote computer terminals, and hyperlinks. Nevertheless, not all e-commerce patents focus upon the use of such technologies. For example, the '127 patent, while generally relating to e-commerce, is not specifically directed toward the Internet. The claims of that patent generally involve a central controller having a CPU and a memory and (at least in some cases) a terminal that is capable of communicating with the central controller, and related operations, but do not recite any web server or other device specifically configured for Internet-type communications. In comparison, the '698 patent is somewhat more clearly directed toward an Internet-type network in at least some of its figures and claims. Nevertheless, that patent and its claims also are not restricted to the use of Internet-type technologies alone.

Also, as discussed above, business method patents need not be limited to processes performed strictly by machines, but rather can include operations performed by human beings. This is evident from the '127 patent and the '698 patent, both of which claim inventions in which human participation is required. For example, claim 4 of the '127 patent recites the steps of inputting departure location criteria and destination location criteria, presumably by a human operator, and claim 30 of the '698 patent recites selection steps being performed by a teacher and multiple students.

These patents therefore suggest that, when attempting to obtain a patent on an e-commerce innovation, you should consider whether your innovation truly needs to be implemented by way of the Internet rather than by way of other communications and/or computer-related technologies, and also consider the extent to which your innovation depends upon human actions as opposed to the operations of computers and other machinery. By considering these issues in view of your understanding as to what already exists in the prior art, you can better prepare (or assist in preparing) claims that provide broad coverage with respect to your innovation without attempting to cover what is already in the prior art.

CHAPTER **4**

Obtaining and Using Your Patent

The following briefly sets forth some of the more important issues that you may face when obtaining and using your patent.

A. Before You Apply for a Patent

The patenting process truly begins before you ever apply for a patent. Because of the patent laws concerning prior art, every new invention is in a time sensitive position as far as the patenting of the invention is concerned. Not only is there always the risk that someone else came up with your invention before you did, but also there is the risk that you will lose your ability to obtain a patent even though you truly were the first inventor—either because of a one-year drop-dead bar date or because you have failed to act diligently in reducing your invention to practice. Particularly problematic is that, in most cases, an inventor will not have complete knowledge of the prior art that threatens the inventor's ability to obtain a patent. In view of these risks, there are a number of important things that you can do or refrain from doing, prior to ever applying for a patent on your innovation, that can improve your chances of obtaining a patent, enhance the value of any patent you eventually obtain, and improve your decision making.

1. Disclosure and Confidentiality Agreements

One of the best things that an inventor or the inventor's company can do to minimize risks associated with prior art is to avoid disclosures and sales (including offers for sale) until a patent application has been filed in the Patent Office. By avoiding prefiling disclosures and sales, the inventor and his company avoid creating drop-dead bar dates based upon their own actions.

Of course, because of business considerations such as the needs of customers, it is not always possible to avoid all disclosures of an invention prior to the filing of a patent application. However, in many of these circumstances it is still possible for an inventor and/or company to protect their ability to obtain a patent despite such disclosures if the disclosures are made under the cover of a confidentiality agreement. That is, limited disclosures made under a properly written confidentiality agreement do not constitute public disclosure.

While effective to some extent, confidentiality agreements are not a panacea. First, confidentiality agreements do not affect the creation of drop-dead bar dates one year later in the U.S. based upon the sale of an invention (or offering of the invention for sale). Also, as with any contractual agreement, there is the possibility that the contract will be breached. While an inventor who has disclosed an invention to another party under a confidentiality agreement can sue the other party in a situation where that other party has failed to keep the disclosed information confidential, the disclosure by the other party may still constitute a disclosure under the patent laws and may consequently prevent the inventor from being able to obtain a patent. Additionally, there are many circumstances in which a confidentiality agreement simply cannot be used, for example, where disclosures must be made to multiple parties in an uncontrolled setting such as a trade show.

2. Recording Your Work

Even if you attempt to avoid public disclosures of your invention prior to filing a patent application, it is almost inevitable that you will eventually become aware of prior art patents and publications, other public disclosures, sales or offers for sale and other forms of prior art that threaten your ability to obtain a patent. It is important that you keep track of the existence of any prior art that has been identified and that you make sure to file a patent application on your invention in time before the prior art deprives you of your ability to obtain a patent.

Since it is usually a patent attorney who will prepare and file your patent application, it is further of great importance that you inform your patent attorney of any prior art of which you are aware, including any disclosures, sales or other actions you have taken that could jeopardize your ability to obtain a patent. A failure to provide this information could result in the invalidation of any patent you eventually obtain, and even create antitrust liability. Ideally, this information should be compiled and summarized on a single form or in a single place (for example, on an invention disclosure form that also summarizes the invention).

Additionally, because the patent law deprives an inventor of the ability to obtain a patent when evidence indicates that another person was actually the first inventor, it is important that you keep accurate and complete records of the times at which you conceived of the invention, improved the invention, built a prototype of the invention, etc. Such records can be critical for establishing that your invention occurred earlier than the times at which other parties independently developed the same invention. Because it can sometimes be complicated to determine who the actual inventors of an invention are, especially in situations involving collaborative teams of engineers or other persons, your records also should specify who contributed what to the invention.

3. Diligence

As discussed above, an inventor who is the first to conceive of a particular invention can in some cases be precluded from obtaining a patent on the invention if the inventor fails to diligently proceed with reducing the invention to practice while another inventor later independently conceives of the invention and proceeds without interruption to reduce the invention to practice. For this reason, an inventor should, whenever possible, diligently proceed with testing the invention and/or pursuing a patent application. Also, an inventor should again keep records (e.g., in a laboratory notebook) concerning the progress being made from the time at which the invention is conceived onward. Such records can help to establish that the inventor has diligently worked to reduce the invention to practice even if the process has taken a relatively long period of time.

4. Prior Art Searches

While an inventor may be aware of some of the prior art that may affect the obtaining of a patent on his or her invention, the inventor is never aware of all prior art. This is problematic, since prior art affects whether an invention can be patented regardless of whether the inventor knows about it, and also because an inventor might change his or her strategy, or even not apply for a patent, if the inventor became aware of certain relevant prior art. Consequently, although there is no requirement that an inventor put forth effort to search for prior art that may be relevant to the invention, it often may be valuable for the inventor to pursue at least some prior art searching.

Ideally, prior art searches would be broad enough to consider all different types of prior art that might potentially affect the patentability of an invention. Yet information concerning some types of prior art, such as information concerning offers of the invention for sale by others, can be nearly impossible to find. In fact, it is often difficult even to identify relevant patents and other publications. Largely this is a linguistic problem, as it is frequently the case that different publications use widely different terms to describe similar technologies, and can be in a variety of foreign languages.

Due to the difficulty of performing prior art or patentability searches, specialized patent and information search firms have emerged, enormous electronic databases of patents and other publications have been compiled, and powerful computer search engines have been developed. Even with the emergence of these specialized firms and search technologies, however, the difficulties associated with searching for prior art remain significant. For this reason, most prior art searches only are capable of providing a general feel for developments occurring in a technology area of interest, and should not be considered as necessarily providing exhaustive reports of the prior art.

Despite these limitations, it is still relatively common for inventors or their companies to perform prior art searches of one type or another (or have prior art searches performed for them), for several reasons. First, even if prior art searches only provide a general feel for the technology area of interest, this information is often sufficient to indicate whether one's supposed invention is actually something that was invented quite a while ago. Second, the search results can be helpful when trying to refine one's invention and determine whether one should attempt to patent specific features of the invention. As discussed above, it is often desirable to obtain a patent to "fill in the gaps" of a technology area, and search results can help one to craft a patent that does this. Generally speaking, prior art searches provide one with information about what is not patentable, which directs one to pursue patent rights that are stronger and more defensible.

Inventors can search for issued patents and patent application publications, which are among the most easily found and understood types of prior art, for free. Specifically, inventors can access and search among United States patent documents stored on the Patent Office database by visiting the Patent Office website (www.uspto.gov). Likewise, inventors can access and search among many foreign patent documents by visiting several other websites (such as www.european-patent-office.org), as well as conduct non-patent literature searches that are standard in their fields.

5. Deciding Whether to Go Ahead

Many times, the business decision concerning whether to pursue patent rights regarding an invention is an easy one. For example, it is clearly appropriate to pursue patent rights concerning an invention if the invention is critical to a company's success and would be easily copied by the company's competitors. In contrast, it is inappropriate to pursue patent rights on an invention if one is already aware of prior art that clearly shows the identical invention. However, in other cases, the decision concerning whether to pursue patent rights is more difficult. In particular, there may be uncertainty over the value of any patent rights that might eventually be obtained. Further, there may be uncertainty about whether an invention is patentable.

Although determining whether to pursue a patent under these circumstances is a judgment call, certain factors do tend to weigh in favor of at least starting the process of obtaining a patent by preparing and filing a patent application. First, assuming that an inventor is unaware of prior art showing the invention and assuming that a prior art search has been conducted before the filing of a patent application on the invention, the author's experience is that it is not that common for previously unknown prior art to arise during prosecution that completely precludes the obtaining of patent rights regarding the invention. Indeed, according to the Patent Office, about two-thirds of all patent applications that are filed in the Patent Office eventually issue as patents.

Second, even if a patent's eventual value is not precisely ascertainable at the start of the patenting process, one should consider that patents can provide value in a variety of ways (as set forth in Chapter 2), and that the value of a patent can be far greater than the relatively limited costs associated with preparing and filing a patent application. Additionally, the patenting process can itself be beneficial insofar as the Patent Office's searching may identify art that is of interest to the applicant for reasons other than merely the patentability of the subject invention, for example, art that bears on products being manufactured and sold by the applicant.

Further, if despite the above considerations one is still uncertain about whether to pursue a patent, one might consider pursuing lower-cost strategies for obtaining patent rights instead of pursuing no patent rights at all. Pursuing patent protection in only one country such as the United States instead of in multiple countries is one way to greatly reduce costs. Moreover, as discussed in the next section, the U.S. patent system allows the filing of a provisional patent application as a way of less expensively filing a patent application and preserving one's patent rights (for a year). Although the filing of a provisional patent application cannot result in a patent without further effort and expense, the filing of a provisional patent application does provide an inventor or company with an additional year to more clearly determine whether it is worthwhile to proceed with obtaining a patent.

B. Applying for a Patent

Although the process for obtaining a patent varies somewhat from invention to invention, the following summarizes the major steps that commonly occur when applying for a patent.

1. Preparation of a Patent Application

The first step in applying for a U.S. patent is to prepare a patent application. This step is usually the most important step in applying for a patent, for several reasons. First, the initial patent application defines the extent of the subject matter of the eventual patent, and new matter cannot be added later without the filing of an additional patent application. Second, the claims in the application set the baseline for the prosecution of the patent application, and significant modification of the claims later on, while possible, can have significant disadvantages. In general, a patent application that is well prepared is more likely to issue (and issue rapidly) as a patent and more likely, upon issuing as a patent, to be enforceable.

a. Choosing What Type of Patent Application to File

The U.S. patent system currently allows an inventor to file, as an original patent application, any of a provisional patent application, a regular (utility) patent application, or a PCT patent application designating the United States. The utility patent application is what is normally filed by U.S. applicants, since a utility patent application starts the prosecution process that can eventually result in a patent, while a provisional patent application without more does not, and an immediate PCT filing significantly delays the prosecution process. Indeed, a provisional patent application must be followed by, or converted into, a utility patent application within one year of the filing date of the provisional patent application in order to avoid abandonment of the patent rights (absent a further delaying step such as filing a PCT patent application that designates the United States).

Given that a provisional patent application cannot by itself mature into a patent, it might initially appear that provisional patent applications serve little purpose. Yet there are circumstances in which filing a provisional patent application makes sense. In particular, because a provisional patent application does not require claims, it can be prepared more quickly than a utility patent application and thus may make sense when it is necessary to file a patent application on short notice, e.g., to beat a bar date. Also, because the preparation and filing of a provisional patent application costs significantly less than the preparation and filing of a utility patent application, the filing of a provisional patent application can afford an inventor a relatively low cost opportunity to protect his or her patent rights and at the same time defer more significant expenses for up to a year. In essence, by filing a provisional patent application, an inventor purchases a one-year option to file a utility patent application (or PCT patent application), which may be particularly valuable when more time is needed to consider the patentability or potential value of an invention.

Filing a provisional patent application instead of immediately filing a utility patent application does have other drawbacks that should be considered when determining what type of patent application to file. In many cases the Patent Office will begin to consider a utility patent application within one year of its being filed. If the Patent Office provides an Office Action (as discussed below) to the patent applicant within that first year, the information provided can be of use to the applicant in getting a better sense of the true patentability and value of the invention. This information can be of value to the applicant in determining whether to invest additional funds into filing foreign patent applications, which normally should be filed within one year of the original U.S. patent application. In contrast, because the filing of a provisional patent application does not start the prosecution process, the filing of a provisional patent application will never by itself result in an Office Action from the Patent Office. Consequently, by filing a provisional patent application rather than immediately filing a utility patent application, an inventor can end up depriving himself or herself of some intelligence that would otherwise be useful in determining whether to pursue foreign patent applications.

Also, to the extent that a provisional patent application is poorly drafted (e.g., because it is prepared in haste), it may later be difficult to rely upon that application's filing date when attempting to avoid the prior art.

b. Preparing the Patent Application

An inventor can prepare a patent application himself or herself. Nevertheless, because numerous legal and technical issues arise during the preparation of a patent application that are most efficiently addressed by someone with experience in preparing patent applications, it is usually recommended that a patent practitioner (e.g., a patent attorney) prepare at least the claims of a patent application and preferably the rest of the document as well.

The basic preparation of a patent application usually involves preparing the drawings and writing the specification, including the claims and abstract (and coming up with a title), although drawings are not always required and claims are not required in the case of a provisional patent application. With respect to patent applications concerning inventions in the mechanical and electrical arts, the drawings typically constitute a very important part of the patent application—in this context, it is often true that "a picture is worth a thousand words." It is a general rule that all claimed mechanical elements be shown somewhere in the drawings, although the clarity with which each limitation needs to be shown can vary significantly.

As for the specification, the length and degree of depth of the specification varies significantly among different patent applications, due to variation in the complexity of different inventions, varying levels of ordinary skill in different technical areas, and many other factors. An important role of a patent attorney in writing a specification is to make sure that it both captures the breadth of an invention and also sets forth the invention in sufficient detail so as to meet the enablement and best mode requirements (discussed in Chapter 1). Often, a patent attorney will do this by describing both the primary embodiment(s) of the invention that are shown in the drawings, and also alternate embodiments that vary in different ways from the primary embodiment(s). To further broaden the scope of the patent, the specification typically also includes somewhere within it a "catch-all" paragraph stating that, while the specification describes certain embodiments of the invention, the described embodiments are only some of a wider variety of embodiments that are part of the invention. Information from other documents can be included within the specification, without including that information word-for-word, by incorporating the documents by reference into the specification.

With respect to the claims, claim writing is a particularly challenging aspect of writing patent applications that is almost always done by skilled patent practitioners. Not only do claims have a specialized format and use many specialized terms (as discussed in Chapter 1), but also good claim writing requires a balance of a number of competing considerations. On the one hand, broad claims are desirable insofar as increased claim breadth results in increased patent rights and patent value. On the other hand, overly broad claims are problematic insofar as it is more likely that the Patent Office will identify prior art that precludes the issuance of those claims or necessitates amendments to the claims. This is undesirable, not simply because it can extend the prosecution process and delay the eventual issuance of a patent, but also because making amendments to claims during prosecution can negatively impact the later interpretation of those claims if the patent becomes the subject of litigation. Further, even if the Patent Office fails to reject overly broad claims, a patent that is issued with such overly broad claims is more likely to be challenged later on as being invalid.

c. Time and Costs of Preparing a Patent Application

The expenses associated with preparing a regular (utility) patent application can vary significantly depending upon a variety of factors, including the technology area of the invention, and the experience of the patent practitioner in dealing with that technology area. In 2004, the preparation of a utility patent application by a patent attorney or agent commonly costs in the range of $6,000–$10,000 for an invention of average complexity, even before governmental and draftsperson's fees are considered. The preparation of an average provisional patent application typically costs less than, and often substantially less than, the preparation of an average utility patent application, since there is typically less effort or no effort put forth in writing claims, there is no need for formal drawings, and fewer associated papers are required in filing a provisional patent application.

2. Prosecution of a Utility Patent Application

In the case of a utility patent application, submission of the patent application to the Patent Office begins a process of persuading the Patent Office that what is claimed in the patent application (or a portion of what is claimed) is a patentable invention deserving of patent protection. The following are some of the major steps in this prosecution process.

a. Filing a Patent Application and Related Formal Documents

Once a patent application has been prepared, it must be filed in the Patent Office in order for the Patent Office to begin its consideration of the patent application. Filing a patent application is important not only because it gets the prosecution ball rolling, but also because (as discussed in Chapter 3) the filing date of a patent application determines whether certain prior art can preclude the patent application from issuing as a patent.

The Patent Office has specific procedures concerning the filing of a patent application. One of the most important of these is the Express Mail procedure, whereby the Patent Office accords a patent application as its filing date the date on which the patent application was deposited in the U.S. mail and sent to the Patent Office using the U.S. Postal Service's Express Mail service. Use of this procedure can be important for a patent applicant when the applicant needs to file a patent application in time to beat a drop-dead bar date. Failure to follow this procedure (e.g., filing by way of a different mail service) means that a patent application will only be accorded as its filing date the date on which the application is physically received by the Patent Office.

Various forms usually accompany a patent application. These include a transmittal form, which summarizes all of the documents being sent to the Patent Office, and a fee transmittal form, on which a patent applicant specifies the fees being paid along with the filing of the patent application. The basic filing fee for a U.S. utility patent application was $790 as of October of 2004, although it increases if the patent application includes more than 20 claims or more than three independent claims, and typically is increased periodically by the Patent Office to keep up with inflation. In comparison, the filing fee for a U.S. provisional patent application was only $160 as of October of 2004. In both cases, the filing fees are further cut in half if the patent applicant is a "small entity," e.g., a small business or an independent inventor. Also typically filed with a utility (but not a provisional) patent application is a declaration (or oath) document. This document is a standard form on which, among other things, the inventor(s) for a patent application attest that they are the true inventors of the inventions in the patent application.

Assignment agreements also are commonly filed along with patent applications when the rights to those applications are being assigned (e.g., to an employer). Typically, to strengthen the legal effect of an assignment agreement, the assignment agreement not only is signed by the inventor(s) but also is notarized and/or signed by witnesses. When filed in the Patent Office, the assignment agreement is accompanied by a recordation cover sheet that summarizes the relevant assignment information for the Patent Office. The submission of assignment documents to the Patent Office is an option, and not a requirement. Assignment documents are commonly submitted to the Patent Office because this allows the Patent Office to record the assignment agreements, which in turn makes it easier later on to prove who owns the subject patent rights, and helps to avoid fraudulent transfers of patent rights. Additionally, when assignment documents are filed, the assignee information can then be listed on a patent that eventually issues.

b. Duty of Disclosure

Persons involved with the filing of a patent application—including inventors, patent attorneys, and all other persons involved with the patent application—must disclose to the Patent Office all information of which those persons are aware that is material to the patentability of the invention in the patent application. This information can include any of the various types of prior art, and should include any information that either establishes on its face (by itself or in combination with other information) that the invention may not be patentable, or contradicts any argument of patentability being advanced by the patent applicant during the prosecution process. The duty of disclosure with respect to a patent application does not end until the application has issued as a patent. An inventor usually acknowledges his or her duty of disclosure when signing the declaration document. Information submitted in accordance with the duty of disclosure is typically submitted by way of a special form called an Information Disclosure Statement (and related PTO Form 1449).

Because there are significant disadvantages associated with not submitting information that is determined after the fact to be material to the patentability of the invention in a patent (e.g., unenforceability of a patent, or possibly an antitrust claim), it is advisable that all information that is even suspected of being material to the patentability of an invention be submitted to the Patent Office. Although the information submitted in accordance with the duty of disclosure sometimes provides ammunition by which a patent application is shot down before it issues as a patent, one should not view compliance with the duty as a burden. Rather, because the strength and value of any issued patent when it is litigated or asserted largely depends upon the degree to which the claims of the patent were properly compared with all existing and relevant prior art, the duty of disclosure actually is beneficial in that it helps to ensure the validity of, and thus serves to increase the value of, issued patents.

c. Standard Prosecution Process

Once a patent application has been filed in the Patent Office, the patent application may sit idle for months and, in some circumstances, even more than a year before the Patent Office begins to consider the patent application. The Patent Office has numerous different art units that examine patent applications dealing with specific technology areas, such that the swiftness of the Patent Office in handling different patent applications can vary significantly for patent applications in different technology areas. Because of the rapid increase in the number of innovations and patent applications in certain rapidly developing technology areas, for example, Internet-related technologies, the delays of the Patent Office in commencing its consideration of patent applications in these areas can be significantly longer than average (currently, up to even three years may pass before the Patent Office begins its consideration of some Internet-related patent applications).

Eventually, a Patent Examiner in a particular art unit picks up the patent application. The Examiner reviews the claims of the application, reviews any related art that the patent applicant has submitted in an Information Disclosure Statement in accordance with the duty of disclosure, and performs an additional search for documents and other art that relate to the invention. As a general rule, the Patent Examiner attempts to identify art that renders the invention in the patent application unpatentable. Also, the Patent Examiner attempts to identify other flaws in the patent application that render the patent application inappropriate for issuance as a patent.

If the Patent Examiner is unable to find anything objectionable about the patent application, the Patent Examiner will allow the patent application to issue as a patent. When this happens, the patent applicant and/or his or her attorney should review the claims in the patent application to make sure that the claims are not more narrow than is necessary to avoid rejection in view of the prior art. Usually, however, the Patent Examiner initially determines that the patent application should not be allowed to issue as a patent due to one or more defects. The Patent Examiner then summarizes his or her rejections/objections in an "Office Action" that the Examiner mails to the patent attorney representing the patent applicant (or possibly to some other party, such as the applicant himself/herself). Upon receiving such an Office Action, the applicant/patent attorney has an opportunity to respond to the arguments of the Patent Examiner in an Office Action response. Typically, three months' time from the mailing date of the Office Action is allotted to the applicant/patent attorney to respond without having to pay additional fees although, by the paying of such a fee, the time for response can often be extended up to six months beyond the original Office Action mailing date.

The response to an Office Action prepared by the applicant/patent attorney can take several different forms. In some situations, the Patent Examiner's arguments are simply wrong or at least arguably wrong, and so the applicant/patent attorney may prepare remarks to rebut the arguments advanced in the Office Action. This occurs more frequently than one might think.

In other situations, the Patent Examiner's arguments have merit, and so the applicant/patent attorney in response amends some portion(s) of the patent application so that the arguments are no longer as pertinent. Often this involves narrowing the scope of one or more of the claims, in order that the claims no longer cover that which is disclosed by prior art. While such amendment of the claims can successfully avoid the prior art, it does have certain disadvantages. In particular, amendments to the claims have the effect that the particular amended words accrue an especially narrow interpretation.

Sometimes, unfortunately (for the patent applicant), the Patent Examiner's arguments are both accurate and all-encompassing to the extent that no reasonable amendment to the patent application can successfully avoid the brunt of the arguments and result in the allowance of meaningful claims. In such circumstances, the applicant may simply give up and not file any response, thus abandoning the application. However, the frequency with which this happens is not that great. Relatively few inventors or companies are willing to invest the resources necessary to pursue a patent application without some sense in advance that what is in the application is inventive. As a result, most patent applications that are filed in the Patent Office tend to have some inventive aspect about them (at least something quite narrow) that is patentable.

Once the applicant/patent attorney has prepared and submitted a response to an Office Action, the ball returns to the court of the Patent Office. The Patent Examiner then has a number of options that he or she can pursue in a subsequent Office Action. Hopefully, for the applicant/patent attorney, the Patent Examiner agrees with the arguments made in the Office Action response and/or agrees that the amendments made by the applicant/patent attorney are sufficient to avoid the earlier grounds for rejection/objection. In such case, the patent application is allowed and proceeds to issue as a patent upon payment of the "issue fee" by the patent applicant.

Of course, the Patent Examiner also may not agree with the applicant/patent attorney. In that case, the Patent Examiner in a new Office

Action may either reiterate the arguments of the previous Office Action or set forth new arguments as to why the patent application is unpatentable. In this way, the argument back and forth between the applicant/patent attorney and the Patent Office can continue, with repeated Office Actions by the Patent Examiner and Office Action responses by the applicant/patent attorney.

While theoretically this argument could carry on forever, the Patent Office does not in practice allow the argument to go on too long. Typically, the second Office Action (or at least one of the third or fourth Office Actions) prepared by a Patent Examiner after the filing of a patent application is categorized as a "final" Office Action. Once the "final" Office Action has been issued, if the applicant/patent attorney fails to successfully convince the Patent Examiner that the patent application should be allowed to issue, the patent application will die unless the applicant/patent attorney takes one of several extraordinary measures.

d. Extraordinary Measures

One way of keeping a patent application alive and keeping the prosecution process going after a final Office Action is by filing a Request for Continued Examination (or RCE). By filing an RCE, which costs a patent applicant the same (or about the same) in terms of governmental fees as the original filing of the utility patent application, the applicant/patent attorney causes the Patent Office to continue the prosecution process. Specifically, the filing of an RCE typically obligates the Patent Office to continue its argument with the applicant/patent attorney for at least two more rounds (assuming that the Patent Office does not change its position and allow the application). That is, typically it will be the second (and sometimes a third or later) Office Action after the filing of an RCE that is again a final Office Action.

An alternative to filing an RCE is simply to file an entirely new patent application, in the form of a continuation patent application that claims priority in the earlier patent application. Upon the filing of such a new patent application (particularly if done in a manner that makes it appear that the new application is somewhat different than the old application), the new patent application may be taken up by a different Patent Examiner than the one handling the earlier patent application. The new Patent Examiner may have a view of the new patent application and the relevant art that is more favorable than that of the earlier Examiner with respect to the earlier patent application, and consequently may be more inclined to allow the new patent application to issue as a patent. This is in contrast to the RCE procedure, in which the prosecution process before and after the RCE filing typically continues before the same Patent Examiner.

Another more involved procedure is to appeal the Patent Examiner's decision to the Board of Patent Appeals and Interferences. The appeal process if pursued to its conclusion will involve the preparation of additional papers such as an appeal brief and/or possibly involve oral arguments before the Board, which can make the process expensive. At the same time, the preparation and submission of an appeal brief can sometimes be an effective way of "calling the bluff" of a Patent Examiner in situations where the Patent Examiner is not very certain that his or her rejections/objections have sufficient merit. That is, sometimes the mere filing of an appeal brief can cause the Patent Examiner to back down and allow the patent application to issue as a patent, particularly if the Patent Examiner wishes to avoid the scrutiny of his or her work that the appeal process would engender or wishes to avoid the burden of preparing documents in favor of his or her position. Although the prosecution process seldom proceeds beyond an appeal to the Board, an applicant can further challenge an unfavorable decision of the Board by appealing to the Federal Circuit.

e. Prosecution History

All arguments, amendments, and other information that arises during the prosecution of a patent application, either due to the actions of the Patent Office or due to the actions of the applicant/patent attorney, constitutes the "prosecution history" (or "file history") of any patent that issues as a result of that prosecution process. Although this prosecution history is not part of what one sees when looking at an issued patent, the prosecution history is a matter of public record that is accessible to the public. Consequently, the prosecution history of a patent constitutes a trail that will inevitably come under scrutiny if and when that patent becomes the subject of litigation.

f. Time and Costs of Prosecution

It is possible for a patent to issue from a patent application even within a year of the filing date of that patent application, particularly in the case where the Patent Examiner allows the patent application upon first considering it. However, much more commonly, the prosecution process involves multiple Office Actions and responses by the applicant/patent attorney, and sometimes can involve one or more of the aforementioned extraordinary measures as well. Consequently, the time required to obtain a patent is often about two years and, in some situations, longer still. The cost of the prosecution process to a patent applicant, following the filing of the patent application, typically is about the same as or less than the cost associated with preparing and filing the patent application, although the cost of prosecution can be higher especially when extraordinary measures such as appeals are pursued.

Of course, one of the key factors affecting the length and cost of prosecution is whether the innovation under consideration is in fact patentable. This can often be the subject of legitimate, complicated debates between the patent applicant and the Patent Office. Yet delays on the part of the Patent Office, particularly delays resulting from excessive backlogs of other patent applications yet to be considered, are another cause of the sluggishness of the prosecution process. Though such delays have occurred throughout the history of the patent system, such delays by the Patent Office are of greater concern today than in the past because the delays frequently occur in new and rapidly changing technology areas, where new technologies can quickly become obsolete. While the new Patent Term Adjustment provisions of AIPA (see Chapter 1) do provide some protection against reductions in patent term that would otherwise occur due to these Patent Office delays, these provisions do not help to eliminate the delays themselves. Nor do the provisional rights established by AIPA necessarily provide applicants with a satisfactory mechanism for recouping what they may lose due to such delays.

3. Important Things to Consider Before Your Patent Is Granted

Once a patent application is allowed, it is normally issued as a patent within a relatively short period of time. Before the patent issues, and preferably prior to payment of the issue fee (typically the last action of the patent applicant before issuance of the patent), there are certain issues a patent applicant should consider.

a. Do You Still Want This Patent?

A first issue that should be considered by the patent applicant before payment of the issue fee is whether the patent applicant still considers the patent to be valuable enough to pursue. As of October of 2004, payment of an issue fee cost $1,370 (half that for a small entity). Consequently, it is worthwhile for a patent applicant to reconsider, upon allowance of a patent application, whether a patent is worth at least the investment of the issue fee. Given the duration of the prosecution process, it is possible that the patent applicant's business priorities may have changed sufficiently such that a patent on the technology claimed in the patent application is no longer valuable. For example, the window of time in which a particular technology has value may have passed. (Of course, if the technology did have value while prosecution was taking place, it may be worthwhile to obtain the patent simply to capitalize on provisional rights that may have arisen due to publication of the patent application).

b. Continuing Patent Applications

Also important to consider before a patent application issues is whether a continuing patent application—either a continuation, a continuation-in-part, or a divisional patent application—should be filed. A continuing patent application can only be filed based upon an earlier patent application so long as the previous patent application is still in prosecution when the continuing patent application is filed. By filing a continuing patent application based upon an earlier patent application before that earlier patent application issues as a patent, one can claim the earlier filing date of the earlier patent application and possibly avoid prior art as a result. However, the earlier filing date only applies with respect to the matter in the continuing patent application that was adequately disclosed in the earlier patent application.

C. Maintaining Your Patent Rights

Once a patent is issued based upon a patent application, the patent is in force. As a general rule, anyone who makes, uses or sells (or imports) the invention as claimed by the patent requires a license to do so and, to the extent that a license is not obtained, one who makes, uses or sells (or imports) the invention infringes the patent. Yet the role of the patent applicant in protecting his or her patent rights does not end with the issuance of the patent. Rather, certain things must be done by a patent-holder following the issuance of his or her patent in order for the patent to remain in force up to the end of its natural lifespan and, additionally, various things can be done by the patent-holder following the issuance of the patent to strengthen the patent.

1. Payment of Maintenance Fees

One thing that must be done by a patent-holder in order to guarantee that his or her utility patent rights remain in force is to pay maintenance fees. Patent maintenance fees are due periodically during the lifespan of a patent—specifically by 3½, 7½, and 11½ years after the patent has issued. If maintenance fees are not paid at these times (or at least within six-month grace periods following these times), the patent becomes abandoned. Upon its abandonment, the patent can only be revived if special conditions are met.

2. Fixing Problems in a Patent by Correction or Reissue

A second thing that can be done by a patent-holder to maintain or strengthen his or her patent rights is to correct the patent or have the patent reissued where appropriate. Sometimes, there may be minor errors in a patent such that the patent could be improved in terms of its clarity if the errors were corrected. In such cases, it makes sense to file a certificate of correction with the Patent Office to attempt to correct such errors.

Further, when there are more significant errors, a patent-holder can in some circumstances request a reissuance of the patent. For example, if new prior art is discovered after the issuance of a patent that clearly renders unpatentable some or all of the claims of the patent, a reissuance of the patent with narrower claim scope can be pursued. Also, if it is discovered that the claims of an issued patent fail to claim the full breadth of the invention due to a misunderstanding on the part of the patent attorney, it is possible to pursue a reissuance of the patent to obtain broader claim coverage (so long as the reissue procedure is begun within two years of the issuance of the original patent). Even if a reissued patent has narrower claims than the original patent, the reissuance of the patent can have beneficial effects upon the patent's value, since the reissued patent is likely of greater strength in view of the prior art than the original patent upon which it was based.

3. Obtaining Reaffirmation of a Patent Through Reexamination

In addition to pursuing the reissuance of a patent, a patent-holder can also pursue "ex parte" reexamination of the patent. The ex parte reexamination procedure provides a mechanism by which the patent-holder can obtain additional affirmation from the Patent Office that the patent is valid in view of patents or publications that were not considered by the Patent Office during prosecution of the patent. This is particularly valuable in circumstances where the patent-holder is having difficulty in asserting its patent against an infringing party because the infringing party is questioning the patent's validity in view of newly identified patents or publications.

The ex parte reexamination procedure is only performed by the Patent Office if the Patent Office initially determines that a substantial new question of patentability has indeed been raised with respect to the patent, as a result of newly identified patents or other publications in the prior art. Other types of prior art that have been identified cannot provide grounds to commence an ex parte reexamination procedure. Assuming that the Patent Office decides that a substantial new question of patentability has been raised and orders a reexamination of a patent, the Patent Office reexamines the patent in much the same way as it initially examined the patent application that became the patent during the prosecution of that application. If during the ex parte reexamination procedure the Patent Office determines that the claims of the originally issued patent are too broad in view of newly identified prior art, the patentee can amend the claims to reduce their scope. However, unlike with respect to the reissue procedure, the claims of a patent cannot be broadened as a result of the ex parte reexamination procedure.

4. Rebutting Challenges to a Patent

That the Patent Office has decided to issue your patent application as a patent creates a powerful legal presumption that your patent is valid in view of the prior art and the criteria for patentability. Despite this presumption, however, third parties can still challenge the validity of your patent and undermine your patent rights, in two ways. First, a third party can challenge the validity of your patent in court. This typically happens in one of two situations—either you have sued the third party for infringement of your patent (or violation of a license agreement concerning your patent), and the third party responds that the patent is invalid, or the third party files a so-called "Declaratory Judgment" action in which the party requests a court to find that your patent is invalid. Defending the validity of your patent in these types of legal actions is very important for protecting your patent rights, since a court decision that your patent is invalid can preclude you from later asserting your patent against third parties who were not even involved with the original legal action.

A second way in which a third party can challenge the validity of your patent is by way of the reexamination procedures. As noted above, one type of reexamination procedure is the ex parte reexamination procedure. While patent-holders, on their own, can seek ex parte reexamination of their patents in order to strengthen their patents, third parties also can initiate the ex parte reexamination procedure. That is, any party can request the ex parte reexamination of an issued patent such that, if the Patent Office determines that a substantial new question of patentability has been raised, a reexamination is performed by the Patent Office. Because of the availability of the ex parte reexamination procedure to third party requesters, there is always the possibility that a patent-holder will have to participate in such a reexamination procedure in order to defend the validity of its patent.

Ex parte reexamination brought about by a third-party requester is relatively friendly to the patent-holder in that the third-party requester does not have many rights to participate in the ex parte reexamination (e.g., following the first submission, the third-party requester has no right to submit arguments as to why the patent is invalid). Consequently, the ex parte reexamination procedure is basically a nonadversarial process for the patent-holder. However, ex parte reexamination is not the only type of reexamination procedure in which a third party can challenge the validity of a patent. Under AIPA, a new form of reexamination procedure termed the "inter partes" reexamination procedure was created that affords a third-party requester much more opportunity to participate in the reexamination process and argue against the patentability of the patent undergoing reexamination.

In particular, during an inter partes reexamination, the third-party requester is allowed the opportunity to comment on responses provided by the patent-holder. Also, the third-party requester has some rights to appeal a decision by the Patent Office to uphold the patent. Consequently, inter partes reexamination can pose a graver threat to a patent-holder's patent, and necessitate greater effort on the part of the patent-holder to defend the patent, than ex parte reexamination. Fortunately for patent-holders, the filing of a request for an inter partes reexamination by a third-party requester is relatively rare, particularly since it is more than three times as expensive as the filing of a request for an ex parte reexamination, and since it still leaves the third-party requester at some procedural disadvantage.

D. Exercising Your Patent Rights

A patent accrues some of its value simply by being issued. For example (as discussed in Chapter 2), some competitors will adjust their operations when they become aware of a patent simply to avoid any accusations of infringement, regardless of whether the patent-holder has any intention of asserting the patent. Nevertheless, patent rights can become especially valuable when they are exercised directly with respect to specific third parties, particularly when a patent-holder asserts a patent against an infringer, or when the patent-holder licenses or sells patent rights to another in exchange for royalties or other payment. The following sets forth some of the issues that should be considered by a patent-holder when exercising its patent rights in these ways.

1. Determining Patent Scope and Infringement

Before a patent is asserted against an infringer, an initial determination should be made by the patent-holder (or its attorney) that the supposedly infringing product(s) or process(es) actually infringe one or more of the patent's claims. Similarly where a patent-holder desires to license or sell patent rights to another, the patent-holder should have a good sense of the scope of its patent claims and what would infringe those claims. There are multiple ways that infringement can occur under the patent law.

a. Claim Coverage and Literal Infringement

One way in which a patent can be infringed is if a party makes, uses or sells (or imports) the invention as exactly claimed in one or more claims of the patent. Such infringement, in which the infringing product or process meets every limitation of one or more of the claims as written, is called literal infringement. Stated another way, a patent is literally infringed if at least one of its claims covers the product(s) or process(es) of the infringer.

b. Infringement Under the Doctrine of Equivalents

The patent law recognizes the imperfection of language, and in particular recognizes that, without an additional "fudge-factor," it would commonly be the case that parties desiring to infringe a patent would attempt to avoid charges of infringement simply by behaving in a way that was only slightly or insubstantially different from the literal meaning of the claims.

To limit the ability of parties to get around the literal scope of a patent's claims simply by taking advantage of the limitations of language, a doctrine known as the "doctrine of equivalents" has developed in the patent law. According to this doctrine, a product or process still infringes a patent claim, even though the product or process does not fulfill every limitation of the claim literally, where the differences between that product or process and the claim limitations are insubstantial. Although the test for determining whether differences are insubstantial can take on a number of forms, one of the most common forms of the test states that the differences between a patent claim and a product/process are insubstantial if the product/process performs substantially the same function, in substantially the same way, with substantially the same result as the claimed invention.

By allowing infringement to be found even when the limitations of a claim are not literally met by the accused product or process, the doctrine of equivalents effectively creates a protective "halo" that broadens the scope of protection created by the claim beyond that defined by the technical, literal language of the claim. Yet the doctrine of equivalents does not stand for the proposition that certain limitations of a claim are unimportant or can be ignored. Rather, the doctrine of equivalents follows the general rule that, in order for a product or process to infringe a claim, the product or process must include each limitation of the claim, or at least an equivalent of each limitation of the claim.

Additionally, the doctrine of equivalents is limited in several ways. Most notable in this regard is the rule that a patent applicant may give up some protection under the doctrine of equivalents if the patent applicant makes an amendment to the claims during prosecution for "a substantial reason related to patentability" (e.g., in order to obtain allowance of the claims following a rejection made in view of the prior art).

c. Contributory Infringement, Inducement and Other Types of Infringement

It is commonly the case that a party will make, use or sell products, or perform processes, that only meet some of the limitations of a claim. While generally such products/processes cannot infringe the claim because the products/processes do not satisfy all of the claim limitations (or equivalents of those limitations), the patent law recognizes that some provision must be made for the situation where one party sells a noninfringing product to another party with the expectation that the other party will use that product in a manner that infringes a patent. Such a provision must be made because, otherwise, there would be no recourse for a patent-holder for infringement in the situation where only the first (selling) party is a legitimate target of an infringement lawsuit (e.g., where the other, receiving party is an end customer). To address this situation, the patent law provides that a party may be held liable for contributory infringement if the party knowingly sells products to another party for the specific purpose of infringing a patent claim (assuming the products have no other substantial, noninfringing use). Likewise, the patent law also provides that parties who induce others to commit infringement are themselves infringers.

Additionally, the patent law also defines infringing behavior to include certain actions that might otherwise be taken by U.S. entities in concert with foreign entities to evade patents. In particular, the patent law provides that parties who supply all of the parts of a patented invention in such a way as to actively induce behavior in foreign countries that would be infringing if performed in the United States also are infringers. Also, it is provided that a party that supplies any component that is especially adapted for use in a patented invention with the intent that the component be combined outside the United States in a manner that would infringe if it occurred within the United States also is an infringer. Further, the patent law provides that a party that imports, sells (or offers to sell) or uses any product in the United States that is made by a process that is patented in the United States infringes the process patent, even if the product was not made in the United States.

2. Licensing, Sale, or Other Transfer of Your Patent Rights

Assuming you believe that one or more claims of your patent encompass subject matter that is of value to another party that is not infringing the patent, it may be financially rewarding to attempt to license, sell or otherwise negotiate a transfer of some or all of your patent rights to that other party. While such efforts are most commonly made in relation to issued patents, in some situations it may also be appropriate to pursue efforts at transfering incipient patent rights such as those associated with a pending patent application.

Approaching a party about licensing or otherwise purchasing your patent rights can sometimes occur by writing a letter to that party and/or arranging a meeting to discuss the transfer of such rights, just as if the patent rights were any other asset being offered for sale. Nevertheless, caution is usually warranted when approaching a party for a possible transaction involving patent rights. In particular, the patent-holder should exercise care to avoid any suggestion that the prospective buyer of the patent rights has already infringed, or has any intention of infringing, any patent(s) at issue. Rather, in this context the goal of the patent-holder should be to convince the prospective buyer that the patent rights and the technology encompassed by those patent rights are valuable for the buyer's business.

Because the successful licensing, sale or other transfer of patent rights to a large extent requires marketing of the patent rights, success largely depends upon the patent-holder's ability to determine the identities and needs of prospective purchasers of the patent rights. It also requires a sense of the reasons why the patent rights may be of particular value to a given purchaser, and the magnitude of such value. Because this information is often difficult to obtain, the transfer of patent rights commonly occurs today in a rather sporadic and inconsistent manner. It remains to be seen whether new techniques or organizations, such as the exchanges mentioned in Chapter 2, or consulting firms, will be able to reduce the informational barriers that continue to hinder the transfer of patent rights.

3. Enforcing Your Patent Rights

If you believe that another party is infringing or likely to be infringing your patent, and you are willing to defend your patent rights, you can proceed with contacting the party to request that the party cease and desist from infringing your patent or request that the party obtain a license to your patent. While some parties will admit the infringement of your patent rights and willingly license or cease violating those patent rights, other parties will refuse to license or cease violating your patent rights even when those parties are clearly infringing your patent. In these circumstances, it may become necessary for you to threaten to sue, or proceed with suing, the infringing party. Of course, such actions and particularly legal suits can become very expensive. However, when determining whether to pursue such legal actions, you as the patent-holder should also consider a variety of other factors, such as the possible damages that could be gained from a favorable court decision or settlement, effects on your reputation in the eyes of competitors depending upon whether you pursue such legal actions, and the possible effects of such actions upon the strength of your patent rights going forward.

Assertion of one's patents in an infringement situation and, particularly, assertion of one's patents in a patent infringement suit are complex undertakings with many strategic aspects, and the details of a patent infringement suit are beyond the scope of the present discussion. Even the initial approaching of a suspected infringer by a patent-holder should be performed with care since, if an overly hostile approach is taken by the patent-holder, the suspected infringer may have grounds to bring a legal action (e.g., a Declaratory Judgment action) against the patent-holder in a nonoptimal forum. Because of the complexity of asserting one's patent against a potentially hostile infringer, and the complexity of patent infringement suits, it is strongly advised that an attorney be hired to handle any patent infringement matter. Nevertheless, some important considerations relating to the assertion of a patent against an infringer are as follows.

a. Notice to Others

In circumstances where a patent-holder has not made, sold, offered for sale or imported products encompassed by its patent, or licensed others to do so, damages may be awarded for infringement of the patent regardless of whether the infringer knew about the patent when the infringement occurred. However, when a patent-holder or its licensee makes, sells, offers for sale or imports products encompassed by the patent, infringement damages only begin to accrue once the infringer has been provided with notice of the patent. For damages to accrue before actual notice is provided by the patent-holder (for example, by initiating an infringement suit or sending an appropriate letter to the infringer), the products encompassed by the patent must be marked to provide constructive notice. To properly mark a product, the word "patent" or the abbreviation "pat.," together with the number of the appropriate patent, should be fixed on the product. When this cannot be done, this information should be provided on a label fixed onto the product or onto a package for the product.

b. The Court System for Patent Matters

As discussed in Chapter 1, U.S. patent infringement actions (as well as Declaratory Judgment actions) are typically first brought in a federal district court, and the decisions of the district courts are appealed to the Federal Circuit. In court, the determination of whether a patent is infringed depends both upon how the patent claims are interpreted and also upon whether the activity of the accused infringer actually infringes the properly interpreted patent claims. Although patent infringement trials in the district courts may be judge or jury trials, the first issue of how to interpret the patent claims is considered to be a "question of law" that is determined by the judge rather than the jury. The exact meaning of the claims is typically argued in so-called "Markman" hearings. Once the claims have been interpreted, the trial than proceeds before the trier of fact (frequently a jury), which determines whether the accused infringer's activities truly infringed the claims of the patent.

c. Laches

One thing to consider if you become aware that someone is infringing your patent is the doctrine of laches. Under this doctrine, if you wait too long to sue for infringement after becoming aware of the infringement, and the accused infringer suffered material prejudice due to your delay, then the accused infringer may have a defense to the charges of infringement. The law provides a presumption in favor of the infringer if six or more years have passed before the patent-holder commenced its lawsuit. Also, a form of the laches defense can be raised with respect to patents that, as patent applications prior to issuance, were in the prosecution process for an excessively long period of time (e.g., decades) due to delays on the part of the patents' applicants.

d. Risks of Patent Litigation

Patent litigation is fraught with risks and uncertainty. Due to many factors—for example, the technical complexity of many patented inventions, as well as relevant prior art, the complexity of most claims, and the continuing evolution of the patent law itself—the central issues of many patent infringement trials can challenge the understanding of the average juror and even some judges. Because of this, as well as because of the ever-present possibility that art from around the world may be found to invalidate the claims of a patent, the outcome of a patent infringement dispute may be difficult to predict, especially prior to comprehensive discovery.

For a patent-holder, the risks of patent litigation include not only the risk of failing to successfully assert its patent against the infringer, but also the risk of not being able to successfully assert its patent against other infringers in the future, particularly when some of the patent claims of the patent-holder's patent are narrowly interpreted or held invalid during the trial. Indeed, the patent-holder in a patent infringement litigation faces the possibility that the accused infringer will successfully argue that the patent-holder's patent is entirely invalid.

Of course, offsetting these risks is the possibility that the patent-holder will obtain a favorable decision. Such a decision may force the infringer to cease its infringing activities or to pay damages. Where the infringement has been willful, the damages can be large, since a finding of willfulness can cause any damage awards to be increased up to three times the original damages. Further, such a favorable decision can provide reaffirmation and strengthening of the patent rights, which can positively impact the patent-holder's dealings with other infringers and with its competitors.

On balance, however, the significant risks and uncertainty associated with patent infringement trials for the patent-holder (as well as the accused infringer) usually make settlement attractive when possible.

Glossary

Absolute novelty: a restrictive rule governing the patentability of inventions in most foreign countries, according to which an inventor must file a patent application prior to publicly disclosing his or her invention to avoid giving up his or her right to obtain a patent on the invention.

AIPA: American Inventors Protection Act of 1999.

Amendment: during the prosecution of a patent application, a submission by a patent applicant in response to an action taken by the Patent Office, in which the applicant requests changes to be made to the patent application.

Apparatus claim: a type of patent claim in which the claim limitations/elements predominantly concern component structures of an overall device.

Appeal: a procedure by which a patent applicant asks a higher authority, such as the Board of Patent Appeals and Interferences, to review and reconsider the decision of a Patent Examiner concerning the patent applicant's patent application during prosecution.

Assignment: a contract in which an owner of a patent (e.g., the inventor) transfers his or her patent rights to another person or entity such as the inventor's employer.

Bar date: a time deadline by which a patent applicant must file a patent application concerning his or her invention in order to avoid losing the ability to obtain a patent on the invention.

Best mode: the most preferred main features or aspects of an invention from the perspective of the inventor, which according to the patent law should be disclosed in a patent application concerning the invention in order for that patent application to issue as a valid patent.

Board of Patent Appeals and Interferences: a board to which appeals are made by patent applicants regarding decisions that have been made by Patent Examiners concerning the applicants' patent applications.

Certificate of correction: an addendum to a patent that is added to the patent after the patent has been issued, which concerns Patent Office printing errors, or minor, non-substantive errors by the applicant (e.g., typos).

Claim: a numbered paragraph at the end of a patent (or at the end of a patent application), which recites limitations that expressly define the invention that is protected by the patent (or, in the case of a patent application, intended to be eventually protected by a patent).

Conception: the primary act of invention, by and at which the inventor(s) become aware of their invention for the first time.

Confidentiality agreement: a contract between a first party and a second party in which the first party agrees not to reveal to third parties information that has been provided to the first party by the second party.

Continuation patent application: a patent application that only discloses the same information that was disclosed in an earlier-filed patent application upon which the continuation patent application is based, and does not disclose new information.

Continuation-in-part patent application: a patent application that discloses new information in addition to that disclosed in an earlier-filed patent application upon which the continuation-in-part patent application is based.

Continuing patent application: one of any of three different types of patent applications (continuation, continuation-in-part, and divisional patent applications) that is based upon an earlier-filed patent application.

Cross-license: a contract between a first party and a second party, in which each party agrees not to sue the other party for infringement of certain respective patent rights.

Declaration: a statement made with respect to a patent application under penalty of perjury, such as the original declaration of inventorship at the time of filing a patent application.

Declaratory Judgment action: a preemptive action that can be brought in federal court by a first party when that party has sufficient reason to believe that a second party is likely to sue the first party for infringement of the second party's patent, and which is typically brought when the first party wishes to obtain a decision concerning the legal merits of the second party's potential suit without waiting for the second party to commence the suit in an unfavorable forum (e.g., a distant court).

Dependent claim: a claim that is based upon at least one other claim in the patent/patent application.

Diligence: with respect to inventions, consistent effort on the part of an inventor or the inventor's agent to develop an invention and reduce it to practice.

Divisional patent application: a patent application that discloses the same information as an earlier-filed patent application, but that typically claims a subset of the inventive subject matter.

Doctrine of equivalents: a patent law doctrine according to which an accused infringer may infringe a claim even if the accused infringer's device or activities are not literally identical to what is recited in the claim, so long as there are only insubstantial differences between the accused infringer's device or activities and what is recited in the claim.

Duty of disclosure: a duty imposed by the patent laws upon inventors, attorneys and others associated with the preparation and prosecution of a patent application to disclose to the Patent Office all information of which any of them are aware that is material to the patentability of the invention being claimed in the patent application.

Enablement: a requirement under the patent law that a patent application describe the invention in sufficient detail that one of ordinary skill in the art to which the invention relates would be able to make and use the invention.

Federal Circuit: the Federal Circuit Court of Appeals.

Filing of a patent application: submission of a patent application to the Patent Office in such a way that the Patent Office is considered to have received the patent application under the patent law.

First inventor's defense: a defense to charges of infringement with respect to business method inventions that is available if the party accused of infringing a patent built the invention claimed in the patent at least one year before the patent was filed in the Patent Office and commercially used the invention before the patent was filed.

Independent claim: a claim that does not refer to another claim.

Information Disclosure Statement: a document that is submitted to the Patent Office in order to attempt to meet the duty of disclosure.

Infringement: making, using, selling, offering to sell, or importing devices, or performing activities, that are encompassed by one or more of the claims (either literally or under the doctrine of equivalents) of another's patent, or acting in certain ways that cause or contribute to others' infringing activities or activities that would be infringing if performed in the United States, when one does not have a license to take such actions.

Intellectual property: forms of property, such as patents and copyrights, which protect intangible assets relating to ideas.

Invention Disclosure Statement: typically, a preliminary description of an invention and related information that is prepared by an inventor for purposes of documenting the invention.

Issuance: the action, taken by the Patent Office, of granting a patent based upon a patent application.

License of patent rights: an agreement not to sue a licensee for infringement of a licensor's patent rights.

Limitation (also element): an identifiable, discrete feature or aspect of an invention as recited in a claim.

Literal infringement: infringement of a patent that occurs when an accused infringer's device or activities are identical to that which is recited in a claim of the patent.

Maintenance fees: fees that must be paid at certain times following the issuance of a utility patent in order for the patent to continue to remain in force until the end of its term.

Marking requirement: a requirement that patent-holders who make, sell, offer to sell, or import devices that are encompassed by their patents mark their devices with information concerning their patents if those patent-holders wish to be able to enforce their patents against would-be infringers for a period prior to the actual notification of those infringers of the existence of the patents.

Markman hearing: an early proceeding within a patent litigation in which the meanings of the claims of the patent at issue are construed by a judge.

Means-plus-function claim: a type of patent claim that employs a special type of language in which structural components are typically recited in terms of their functions.

Method claim: a type of patent claim in which the claim limitations predominantly concern operations or functions that are performed in accordance with the invention.

Nonobviousness: a test of inventiveness (more demanding than novelty) that depends upon several factors including the teachings of the prior art, the level of ordinary skill in the technology art of the invention, and various secondary factors.

Notice: notification that a patent exists with reference to a particular product, which can be either actual or constructive.

Novelty: a test of inventiveness that depends upon whether all of the limitations of a claimed invention can be found in a single prior art reference.

Office Action: an action taken by the Patent Office during the prosecution of a patent application.

Ordinary skill in the art: an idealized level of skill of an average technologist in a particular technology area.

Patent: a document that defines the scope of patent rights to exclude others from making, using, or selling (or offering to sell or importing) an invention that is claimed in that document.

Patent application: a document that describes and (except in the case of some provisional patent applications) claims an invention and, when filed in the Patent Office, can eventually issue as a patent without any additional patent application filing or conversion process (except in the case of provisional patent applications).

Patent application publication: a document that may be published showing the contents of a patent application.

Patentable subject matter: the types of inventions that can be patented in accordance with the patent laws.

Patentability: the issue of whether a particular idea can be patented or not.

Patent portfolio: a group of patents, often concerning related inventions in the same or similar technology areas.

Patent Term Adjustment (PTA): changing of the term of a patent based upon actions/delays of the Patent Office and the patent applicant during prosecution.

PCT: the Patent Cooperation Treaty, which among other things provides a standardized process for filing patent applications in many countries.

Preamble: the first, introductory phrase or clause of a claim.

Prior art: any of a variety of documents or other types of information that, in accordance with the patent law, can be considered when determining whether an invention is patentable or not.

Prosecution: the process of interaction between a patent applicant and the Patent Office between the time a patent application is filed and the time it issues as a patent, during which the Patent Office determines whether the invention claimed in the patent application is patentable and whether the patent application meets other requirements for being patented.

Prosecution history/file history: the patent application, Office Actions, amendments, correspondence and other documentation that comes into existence during the prosecution of a patent application and serves as a record of that prosecution.

Provisional patent application: a special, less-expensive type of patent application that does not require claims, that cannot by itself issue as a patent, and that can only eventually result in a patent if the patent applicant takes an additional action (filing another patent application or causing a conversion process to occur) within a year after the application is filed in the Patent Office.

Provisional rights: in accordance with AIPA, special rights of a patent-holder to receive royalty payments from other parties concerning their behavior between the time the patent-holder's patent was issued and the earlier time at which a patent application publication relating to that patent was published.

Reduction to practice: usually, either the act of successfully implementing/testing an invention or the act of filing a patent application that fully discloses a workable embodiment of the invention.

Reexamination (ex parte or inter partes): proceedings before the Patent Office by which a patent may be reconsidered with respect to the patentability of the invention claimed in the patent.

Reissue proceeding: a proceeding before the Patent Office by which a patent is withdrawn and prosecution of the underlying patent application is reperformed, in order to allow for correction of an error that occurred during the original prosecution of the patent application.

Request for Continued Examination (RCE): an action that can be taken by a patent applicant in order to cause the prosecution of a patent application to continue even after the Patent Office has made a final rejection of the patent application.

Secondary considerations: certain additional factors that can influence a determination of nonobviousness.

Specification: the main textual portion of a patent application or patent.

Utility: the test of whether or not an invention is useful.

Utility patent: a patent that concerns an invention that relates to a process, machine, manufacture or composition of matter, and that has a practical use.

Validity: the issue of whether a patent is valid, which depends upon both whether the tests of patentability have been met, as well as whether the patent meets various other technical criteria.

About the Author

John T. Pienkos is a registered patent attorney who practices intellectual property law at Quarles & Brady LLP in Milwaukee, Wisconsin. He earned a B.S. in Electrical Engineering from Marquette University and a M.S. in Electrical Engineering from the University of Wisconsin—Madison, where he pursued research in the area of microwave heating of plasmas for nuclear fusion. Mr. Pienkos earned his J.D. from Harvard Law School in 1997. He serves as co-chair of the Wisconsin chapter of the Licensing Executives Society, which he co-founded.